Get Organized TODAY

Top experts share strategies that work

Power Dynamics
PUBLISHING

PowerDynamics Publishing
San Francisco, California
www.powerdynamicspub.com

ISBN: 978-0-9644906-5-9

Library of Congress Control Number: 2010928394

Printed in the United States of America on acid-free paper.

We dedicate this **book**

*to you, the business owner, the householder,
the parent, the daughter or son
who recognizes the power of having
your inner and outer life ordered in a way
that brings peace of mind and clarity of being.
We salute you for embracing the
power of organization in your life—
and we celebrate your commitment
to being the best you can be!*

The Co-Authors of *Get Organized Today*

Table of **Contents**

Acknowledgements

Gratitude is an essential element in organizing one's thoughts and highest intentions for others. Before we share our wisdom and experience with you, we have a few people to thank for turning our vision for this book into a reality.

This book is the brilliant concept of Caterina Rando, the founder of PowerDynamics Publishing and a respected business strategist, with whom many of us have worked to grow our businesses. Working closely with many organizing professionals, Caterina realized how much she was learning about organizing and arranging one's life in a way that enhances one's inner and outer world. The result was putting these ideas into a comprehensive book.

Without Caterina's "take action" spirit, her positive attitude and her commitment to excellence, you would not be reading this book, of which we are all so proud.

Additionally, all of our efforts were supported by a truly dedicated team who worked diligently to put together the best possible book for you. We are truly grateful for everyone's stellar contribution.

To Ruth Schwartz, with her many years of experience and wisdom, who served as an ongoing guide throughout the project, your leadership and support to our production team is deeply appreciated.

To Erin Sarika Delaney, whose care in working with the co-authors and copyediting their work proved incredibly valuable and ensured that this book would be the best it could be.

To Tammy Tribble, who brought her creative talent to the cover design, and Barbara McDonald, who brought her brilliance to the design and layout of the book, thank you for your enthusiasm, problem-solving and exquisite attention to detail.

To both Bernie Burson and Karen Gargiulo, who provided us with their keen eyes and their elegant touch, thank you for your support and contribution.

To co-author Angela Wallace, who provided insight and advice throughout the project, thank you for sharing your wisdom and knowledge.

We also acknowledge each other for delivering outstanding information, guidance and advice. Through our work in this book and with our clients, we are truly committed to enhancing the lives of others through the use of organization. We are truly grateful that we get to do work that we love and make a contribution to so many in the process. We do not take our good fortune lightly. We are clear in our mission—to make a genuine contribution to you, the reader. Thank you for granting us this extraordinary opportunity.

The Co-Authors of *Get Organized Today*

Introduction

Congratulations! You have opened an incredible resource, packed with great ideas that will enhance your life in ways you cannot yet imagine. You are about to discover the magic of how to *get organized today.*

The success of your personal and professional life comes as the result of more than talent, commitment and hard work. Your success will also be determined by how you organize your life—your home, your office, your relationships—to meet the needs of a demanding world. In fact, your success is determined by the way you arrange and sort all of the important aspects of your life. We know you want to be the absolute best you can be.

With this book, you can quickly learn how leaders in the organizing field can assist you in organizing the various areas of your life to gain peace of mind. As top experts in each of our respective specialties, we've joined together to give you powerful organizing information and strategies. Each of us has seen how even small changes in order and organization can transform and uplift your life.

All the organizing professionals you will meet in this book want you to live your life with ease and simplicity. We have outlined for you our top tips and included the most expert advice we have to enhance your life.

Some of the ideas we want to share with you include:

- Knowing how to conquer your piles of paper and other challenges in your home and office offers you the opportunity to accomplish more.
- Eliminating the clutter from your life in an eco-friendly way not only benefits you, it also benefits the planet.
- Preparing for possible disasters in an orderly manner will help provide you with peace of mind, knowing you will be ready for the unexpected.

To get the most out of *Get Organized Today,* we recommend that you read through it once, cover to cover. Then go back and follow the advice that applies to you in the chapters most relevant to your current situation.

Every organizational improvement you make will impact how you feel about yourself and how you perform your work in the world. It will also make a difference in the lives of those around you.

Know that just learning what to do will not transform your life. You must take action and apply the strategies, tips and tactics we share in these pages in order to reap the many rewards. With our knowledge and your action, we are confident that, like our thousands of satisfied clients, you too will master the magic of knowing how to *get organized today.*

To your boundless success!

The Co-Authors of *Get Organized Today*

Capturing the **Vision**
Creating a Space You'll Love

By Rhonda Elliott

Congratulations! You've decided you are going to organize that cluttered space and make it a place where you'll love spending more time. The "space" can be a small corner nook or your entire house. And now here come those dreaded words that have crossed your lips before, "It's all so overwhelming—I have no clue where to start."

You are not alone. Most everyone finds the task of getting organized extremely overwhelming and daunting at first. We all dream of turning a cluttered, uninviting space into a warm, welcoming place in which we spend more time. We know that creating a beautiful place for our daily living makes a tremendous difference in the quality of our lives. One obstacle holds most people back— the lack of a clear vision for the space.

"If you can dream it, you can do it."
—Walt Disney, American film producer, animator, entertainer

The old saying, "You can't see the forest for the trees," reminds us that we are often too close to the problem to see new possibilities. In this chapter, I offer you the best tips and ideas that I share with my clients. An advantage I have as a professional organizer is the ability to enter my client's space with a fresh perspective, carrying no preconceived notions or judgments of how things *should* be. To let you in on a secret, I don't even see the clutter—I only see possibilities. My role is two-fold: to help my clients create their vision and then help them capture their vision so it can become a reality.

Are you struggling to create your vision? Or, perhaps you have a vague vision, but you're puzzled about how to bring it to reality? My passion is watching my clients move from feelings of overwhelm to feelings of pure joy and excitement when they capture the vision and know how to bring it to life. I will be your personal organizing coach, so you, too, can move from overwhelm to excitement as you create, capture and bring your vision to life. Give yourself permission to dream big as you build this vision. I promise you'll even have fun along the way.

Creating Your Vision

The sky is the limit—let your imagination run wild. As small children, we were encouraged to let our imaginations take flight and soar. The books we read were filled with beautiful pictures and exciting adventures. Unfortunately, as we grew older and had to live in the "real world," our imaginations were often pushed aside. Well, during the creating-your-vision process, I encourage you to bring

2

imagination back to front and center. It is only when we give free rein to our dreams that we begin to see new possibilities.

> *"The real voyage of discovery consists not in seeking new landscapes, but in having new eyes."*
> —Marcel Proust, French novelist, critic and essayist

Creating a "my vision" notebook. Going through this vision-creating process, you may want to set up a place to collect all your inspirations: pictures, ideas, sketches, articles and so on. Having a home to organize your thoughts—your inner space—makes organizing your physical space so much easier. One possibility is to create a three-ring "My Vision" binder. Fill the binder with writing paper to record your thoughts and ideas and plastic sheet protectors to hold pictures and articles. Divide the binder into five sections: Purpose, Inspiration, Theme, Mood, and Action Plan. These sections are described in further detail throughout this chapter. If you're computer-savvy, you can collect this information into an online folder.

Looking at the big picture. I am always fascinated by how things appear differently when I'm looking out an airplane window, flying above a city. Feeling removed and above the fray, buildings, roads and even traffic take on a totally different perspective.

You can get this same new perspective when you view your cluttered space "from above." Picture the space empty. What special architectural features does the space offer? Consider the size of the space, door and window placement, the natural traffic flow, which objects are permanent and which ones can be moved.

3

Giving the space a purpose and intention. My favorite questions to ask clients are, "How do you want to use this space?" and "What is motivating you to get this space organized?" Is the space going to be a calm, restful sanctuary where you can escape from a frenzied world? Or a fun-filled game room for the family and guests? Maybe you want a place to enjoy a hobby without having to clean up the mess each time or perhaps a study hall for the kids. In the Purpose section of your notebook, describe in as much detail how you see this space being used and why this is important to you. The more precise you are, the clearer your vision becomes and the sooner it becomes reality.

> *"Our intention creates our reality."*
> —Dr. Wayne Dyer, American motivational speaker and author

Refining Your Vision

Now that you have a sense of the big picture and purpose for your space, you can begin refining that vision—this is where the fun really begins. You will need to use your powers of observation and imagination.

Finding inspiration. The good news is that inspiration is all around you. Everywhere you look holds new ideas. What are you passionate about? How do you enjoy spending your free time? What makes your heart sing? Here are some places to get you started and you can add others as you think of them:

Magazines	**Your hobbies**	**Favorite keepsakes**
Design books	**TV shows**	**Design websites/blogs**
Favorite stores	**Movies**	**Your travels**
Gardens	**Flea markets**	

At this stage of the process, ignore the cost of items—just let everything inspire you. Remember, you don't have to spend a lot of money to create a beautiful space; it just takes using things that bring you joy!

Collect pictures and photos that inspire you. Also, write down ideas or quotes that spark your imagination. Store all these great ideas in the Inspiration section of your notebook.

"Inspiration is all around us. If you take an active role in your life, you will find it."
—Bruno Baceli, American motivational speaker and author

Choosing a theme on which to build. As you gather your inspiring pictures and ideas, you will begin to see a pattern—a common thread. This pattern helps lead you to a theme for the space.

A client's grown daughter was coming for a visit and staying in her mother's master bedroom. The bedroom definitely needed de-cluttering and freshening up. As we began to sort through her things, I heard my client repeat several times that certain items were small gifts for her daughter. I suggested we create a gift basket similar to what fancy hotels offer their guests. That sparked my client to ask if she could put a chocolate on the pillow. "Of course," I answered, "isn't this a five-star hotel?" And, in that moment, a hotel theme was born. The space now had a clear vision and the rest of the day was a breeze. The best reward, though, came when the daughter arrived that evening. My client reported that her daughter was so delighted and will never forget her visit!

Focusing on your space and its purpose can be highly enjoyable. Adults learn from reference points—things they already know. Say to yourself "spa retreat" and your brain instantly conjures up a calm and serene image. If you want to create a quiet reading niche, perhaps a cozy English library can be your theme. Your pantry can be fashioned after your favorite gourmet market. You get the idea.

Study your inspiration pages and let a theme emerge. Themes are powerful and very motivating. Write down your theme in full detail in the Theme section of your notebook.

Choosing the desired mood and impression. Now that you have a theme, it's time to decide on the mood and impression you want the space to convey. Setting the mood and impression will help you determine how to organize the space. To decide on a mood, ask yourself how you want to feel when you're in this space. Do you want the space to be a serene sanctuary? Or do you want it to be a bright, warm, inviting place filled with family, friends, and your favorite things?

Lighting and color help create a mood. Lighting has three main types: general, task, and accent. Each has its own specific purpose. General lighting, sometimes called ambient, provides the overall illumination of the space. Natural lighting contributes to general lighting. Task lighting adds additional lighting for specific tasks such as reading, cooking, etc. Accent lighting adds drama and visual interest.

Colors also help set the mood of a room. We see colors with our emotions, not our heads. Because of this, colors have the power to put us in a variety of moods. Warm colors invite you into a room with their coziness, while cool colors have a calming effect. For example, if you want your family room to be a welcoming, lively and energetic space, use reds, yellows or oranges. If you are creating a calm bedroom retreat, use blues, browns or greens. A fresh coat of paint is a quick and inexpensive way to alter the mood of a room.

Consider the type of mood you want your space to convey. Describe it in the Mood section of your notebook.

Personalizing Your Vision

> *"Have nothing in your house that you do not know to be useful,*
> *or believe to be beautiful."*
> —William Morris, 19th century British craftsman and designer

Now that you have an overall sense of your vision, you can more easily decide which items belong in the space and which ones do not. As you begin to build your space, first think of your exact need and then look closely at what you have and see if it can be given a new purpose.

- **Adding your personal touches.** Make your space a reflection of you— your interests, hobbies, collections, travel mementos, photos, artwork, fresh plants and flowers—even your sense of humor. Surrounding yourself with personal treasures can bring immense joy.

- **Shopping from your own items first.** Before I meet with new clients, I urge them not to go out and buy any new items. This can range from small items such as file folders or baskets to large items such as furniture. I assure them that shopping from what they already have may save them money. You may find that a lamp in another area, or even in storage, fits into your vision for a new space.

- **Putting each item to the test.** One of the most challenging parts of getting organized is figuring out what to do with each item currently in the space. With your newly defined vision in mind, the decision becomes easier to make. You simply ask yourself: does this item enhance the vision or detract from it? If the item enhances the vision, it gets to stay. If not, it has to go—to another room, to a charity, to the recycle bin, wherever.

- **Repurposing items to get more "bang for your buck."** Capturing your dream doesn't mean you have to buy all new things for your space. Just because an item was designed for one purpose doesn't mean it can't be used in a different way. I have a client who repurposed an old wooden doll cradle from her childhood to hold bottled beverages on her patio. Now each time she grabs a soda, she has a happy memory. As an added bonus, she saved money by not buying a new drink container.

As you begin to build your space, first think of your exact need and then look closely at what you have and see if it can be given a new purpose.

Capturing Your Vision and Bringing It to Life!

"Knowing is not enough; we must apply.
Willing is not enough, we must do."
—Goethe, 18th century German poet, author, philosopher

Aha! You have captured your vision. Now you can create the space you love. Simply break the organizing process into small logical steps. Write these steps down and store them in the final section in the "My Vision" notebook. This is your Action Plan—it provides you with a sense of direction to reach your desired goal. Enjoy your new space!

RHONDA ELLIOTT
Organized By Design

*Providing creative solutions
to satisfied clients since 1994*

(925) 426-9540
rhonda@organizedbydesign.biz
www.organizedbydesign.biz

Rhonda has always had a passion for well-designed and organized spaces. As a young girl, Rhonda delighted in making her bedroom a cherished space, as well as helping her girlfriends beautify their bedrooms. Throughout her career in the high-tech computer world, Rhonda applied her organizing and design skills to help her corporate clients create data systems, which greatly improved their productivity.

By 1994, Rhonda was ready to use her passion in a more creative way again and launched her company, Organized By Design, in Pleasanton, California. She brings enthusiasm, creativity, and non-judgmental support to help her clients visualize and create an environment that meets their specific needs and preferences. Rhonda's clients range from individuals to small businesses to large corporations. Her extensive organizing and design skills include residential organizing, space design, office organizing, system design, time and paper management and clutter control.

Rhonda has been an active member of the National Association of Professional Organizers (NAPO) at both the local chapter (San Francisco Bay Area) and the national level since 1994. She delivers organizing workshops and is a compassionate and dynamic speaker to professional and service organizations.

The Organizing **Triangle**
Three Essential Points to Get and Stay Organized

By Charlotte Steill, CPO®

It is my sincere belief that a home should lift your spirits when you walk through the front door, be a sanctuary from the outside world and alleviate stress rather than contribute to it. Over the years, I have been privileged to work with many clients to help them achieve this end.

There are many types of disorder that can cause your home to add stress to your life. Some homes have surfaces covered with clutter, while others, at first glance, look perfect but disorder can be found in each cabinet, drawer and closet. In both cases, the home has simply become undefined. The one word most of my clients use to describe their environment before we organize is *overwhelming*. They feel as though they just don't know where to start. It is hard to put things away when you have no idea where they belong. It can happen to any of us. Life gets busy or we encounter a major life transition and before we know it our environments are off balance.

I have worked side by side with these individuals to define the spaces in their homes and create lasting change that they can maintain easily. I am honored to share with you what I have taught and what I have learned.

Early on, I realized that complicated approaches to organizing often lead to unfinished projects and a sense of failure. For this reason, I developed the Organizing Triangle, a simple strategy to get and stay organized.

The Organizing Triangle

All triangles have three points—two that create the base or foundation and one that is the pinnacle or top point, which often directs us to a specific destination. In the Organizing Triangle, I name the two base or foundational points *systems* and *products* and I name the pinnacle or top point *habits*. These new habits will point you toward lasting change. Always keep these three things in mind when dealing with disorganization. If, after you organize, your home begins to feel undefined or out of balance, simply follow the points to restore order to any space. These are the three essential components to get and stay organized.

> *"We should learn from the snail.*
> *He has devised a home that is both exquisite and functional."*
> —Frank Lloyd Wright, American architect

Organizing Triangle Point #1: Systems

A good definition of *system* is this: due method or orderly manner of arrangement or procedure. Creating systems is the first point of the triangle and essential to maintaining any organized space. Systems keep things running smoothly. Our world and our body rely on systems we rarely think about: our solar system, our eco-system, our circulatory system and so on. Well-planned systems require little thought to maintain. Our vehicles have systems to keep them running and when the system is close to breaking down, a warning light comes on to signal us it needs our attention. A system, as it applies to organizing, is identifying what is important in your life and making it accessible. The warning light comes on when a space is so full nothing else can fit in it. That is the cue that that space needs attention.

Setting goals. Before you can create a system, it is absolutely necessary to plan and set goals. Visualize how you want your home to look and how you would like it to function. You will need a journal or a spiral notebook to capture your thoughts and ideas. Devote the notebook to your project and keep it handy. Write down a general vision of the end result you would like to achieve. Devote a page in your journal for each space you would like to organize and write a specific goal and vision for that room. For example, a goal for your bathroom might be to eliminate all the old products lurking under the sink or in the cabinets and create a better storage system for toiletries to avoid overbuying.

Here are two key questions to answer in order to begin to create a system that will benefit you and fit your life:

1. Who are you? It's important to know what your likes and dislikes are. It is easy to get so involved in the business of everyday life that you forget to make time or even think about who you are and what it is that brings you joy. If you could have a perfect living space, what would it look like and how do you see yourself living in it? Do you need to have things visible in order to know where they are? Do you like to have clear surfaces or are you a collector of knick-knacks? What is your favorite color? What is your decorating style? Which decorating style do you admire? If you live with others, are you willing to pick up after them or do you want everyone to pitch in? Are you a morning person or a night owl? Write down the answers to these questions along with anything else you feel might be pertinent to you in your home environment. It is also a must to note any habits you or your family have that contribute to disorder. For instance, do you put purchases away as soon as you get home or do you leave them in their bags to do later? Do you or your spouse tend to save junk mail and periodicals to look at later? Do you pick up clutter and hide it when guests come over?

2.What is your lifestyle? Are you a working person? Retired? Do you have children at home? Are they young? Teens? Are you home more than you're out or out more than you are home? Do you entertain? How often? Are you involved in sports? Do you collect things? It is important to identify what your lifestyle is like to determine what things you need to support that lifestyle.

Evaluating your belongings. I have heard two definitions of clutter that have resonated with me. The first one is that clutter is simply something that doesn't have a home. I could not agree more with this. The second definition is that clutter is a delayed decision. This is one that really made me think and also the one I talk most about with my clients. How do you think this might apply to you? Do you often let something go because you do not feel like making or are afraid to make a decision? I believe that fear stems from the fact that we really haven't taken the time to think it through. Before you start to organize, it is crucial that you identify the things you need to support your current life. Not the things you needed in the past or the things you might need in the future.

Clearing the clutter. Clearing the clutter can be a daunting task for some. For more on clearing clutter from your environment, see Nancy Castelli's chapter, *Get Organized for the Planet,* on page 183. My clutter clearing advice is simple and methodical. If you don't have time for a huge organizing project, you can easily incorporate this habit into your daily life. Here are my simple steps.

14

1. Create a donation receptacle. This can be a large trashcan lined with a bag, a box or a shopping bag. Whatever you choose, just make sure it's handy and in a designated area.

2. Follow the ten-in-ten rule. Create a daily ritual of clearing ten things in ten minutes. Choose the time of day when you have the most energy and set a timer to keep you on track. You can focus on one room, drawer, cabinet or closet at a time or just wander the house looking for the ten things that are no longer useful to you. Whether it is paper, broken items, expired food or clothes that don't fit, the goal is to throw away, donate or recycle ten things each day. You will be amazed at how your space transforms when clutter is eliminated.

3. Identify a person or place that you deem a worthy recipient of your cast-offs. If you choose a charity, trust that the charity to which you donate will be a good steward of your donations. Try not to worry where the thing you have let go of will end up. Believe that things end up finding their way to the right recipient.

My daughter and I have a friend who is not as fortunate materially as we are. We keep a shopping bag handy to catch anything we no longer need or want. At least twice a month, we send bags of goods off to our friend and she either uses them herself or shares them with her community. Many useful things leave our home on a regular basis and still we live in abundance. Don't be afraid to let go of the old, as the new will always appear.

4. Find a place for everything. After you have eliminated all the excess clutter in your home, it's time to think of where the things you use will live. Remember, clutter is something that doesn't have a home. Your next task is to create homes for everything you keep. Assign a specific function for each drawer, closet, shelf, nook and cranny in your home. Undefined spaces attract piles! The trick to deciding where things should be located is to consider where they are used. Place the items you use often in the most convenient spaces and seldom-used items out of reach.

Organizing Triangle Point #2: Products

Products are a vital part of getting and staying organized. Products create homes for things. For example, a hanging file is a product that creates a home for a category of paper. Many files together create a filing system. In working with clients over the years, I have noticed that a lot of organizing products are purchased because they are attractive and then become part of the clutter. They lay abandoned on desktops, closets and pantries and at their worst, they become clutter catchers—filled with things that have been long forgotten.

Organizing has become very popular and there are a myriad of products that promise to be a cure for your chaos. Don't be drawn in by looks alone. Although there are many pretty organizing products that work, it is generally the most basic of the products that are the backbone of any system. Here are some items I have found incredibly important to have on hand to implement a solid organizing system:

1. Shoeboxes. These are so handy in the initial organizing process to sort items into groups of like kinds and then to store things in for the long term. I use labeled plastic shoeboxes to hold all of my office supplies and craft supplies. I also use them to make what I call K.I.T.S. (keep it together simply). I have kits for jewelry cleaning supplies, shoe repair, sewing supplies, extension cords, spice packets and so many other things.

2. Larger bins. These are great for clothing, holiday decorations, gardening supplies and so on. Plastic bins are essential, as you can easily label and store them. Keep in mind that odd-shaped bins will not work as well as true rectangular bins. Be sure to buy several bins at once rather than buying one here and there. Bins must be of the same shape and size in order to build a system that will work over time.

3. Drawer organizers. These come in all different sizes and materials to fit any drawer in your home. Install enough organizers to fill the drawer completely. Use a product called museum gel to stick them down and prevent wandering. Drawer organizers are a must for corralling like items together from kitchen gadgets to makeup, office supplies to tools.

When organizing a room, it helps to have these three essentials on hand. Use them first for sorting and then for containing. Don't forget to label your bins. Clear labels from electronic label makers are great for labeling the inside of drawers and the edge of shelves. Labels become visual cues that remind you that things have specific homes. They also aid in creating the habits needed to maintain order.

These are the only products from which you will benefit by buying in advance. Resist buying anything else until you are putting the finishing and aesthetic touches on the organized space. A good rule of thumb for deciding how many products to buy is to measure your shelves and cabinets and purchase enough products to fill the space, giving yourself room to grow.

"We are what we repeatedly do.
Excellence then, is not an act, but a habit."
—Aristotle, Greek philosopher

Organizing Triangle Point #3: Habits

Habits are at the top of the organizing triangle, as they are the actions that point us in the direction of lasting change. Don't expect perfection overnight. New habits take time to establish. The following are examples of habits that will help you maintain the organization you have achieved:

* **Put things back where they belong.** Now that everything has a home, resist placing things on the first available surface. If you are busy and it's impossible to put things away at the time of use, then take ten minutes each night to put everything away.

* **Edit items on a regular basis.** Organizing is not a one-time event. It is a lifestyle that requires continual evaluation. When a home you have created is overflowing, it's time to take a look at the contents. Are you overbuying or do some of the older things need to be donated or recycled? Regular assessments will give you the answer.

* **Take the phrase "I'll do it later" out of your vocabulary.** In my experience, it is not the things we do that wear us out, it is the things that are left undone.

The rewards of an organized lifestyle are many. Organization saves money by helping you avoid buying duplicates. It saves time by giving you the ability to find the things you need when you need them and it brings peace of mind in a stressful world. Organized spaces simply feel better. They give you and your loved ones peace of mind, room to breathe and time for what's important. You have your three points to getting and staying organized. Now it is time to get started on your systems, products and habits for an organized home.

CHARLOTTE STEILL, CPO®
Simply Put Organizing

(480) 659-2663
charlotte@simplyputorganizing.com
www.simplyputorganizing.com

Charlotte began her organizing business in 2001. She is a member of the National Association of Professional Organizers (NAPO) and the past president of the Arizona Chapter. Having worked professionally for the required number of hours and passing the inaugural certification exam administered by the Board of Certified Professional Organizers, Charlotte was one of the first three organizers in Arizona to receive the prestigious title of Certified Professional Organizer, CPO. Charlotte is a nationally recognized television personality, having been a guest on HGTV's *Mission Organization,* and appears locally each month on ABC's *Sonoran Living Live.* She frequently shares her organizing insights with magazines and newspapers nationwide.

Charlotte's experience in corporate America as well as her life as a single working mom has taught her the value of good organizing habits. She combines her real world experience with her God-given abilities to customize systems that restore order and fit each client's unique needs.

Charlotte operates according to the philosophy that simple systems, combined with eye-appealing design and new habits, will transform a space, creating lasting change easily maintained by her clients.

Create a **Productive** Environment in Five Steps

By Sandy Stelter, JD, CPO®

We, as human beings, generally want to feel productive and be productive. We want to be able to find things when we need them and get to appointments, meetings, school or work on time. We want to know that we can easily locate last week's article on the best vacation places in America or the email we saw just yesterday that contained an address we need now.

> *"A productive environment is a setting in which everything around you supports your goals and who you want to be."*
> —Barbara Hemphill, CPO, productivity expert, speaker, author

When we allow disorganization and clutter to overwhelm our lives, we lose sight of our goals, begin to feel overwhelmed and start to spin our wheels. We have difficulty setting and maintaining our priorities. We constantly find ourselves with too much to do and too little time to do it. Free time, what's that? Even recreation becomes another thing "to do." Deadlines can cancel recreation easily. Only illness, maybe, slows us down. Work piles up, small tasks become overwhelming and we see clutter everywhere we look. How can we possibly be productive living this way?

Each of us pays a price for our disorganization and the resulting lack of productivity in terms of the following:

- **Money.** Money leaks out because you have to pay late charges for the misplaced bills or you must buy items that you know you already have...somewhere. The costs add up.

- **Space.** Stacks of paper, clutter and other non-essentials accumulate because you are inundated with information you can't readily access or dispose of.

- **Time.** You are always late getting out of the house, never seem to be able to catch up and cannot seem to focus on your priorities.

- **Energy.** The mental stress of missing deadlines and spending precious time looking for the appointment information, the car keys or the document you need is exhausting and unproductive.

It is difficult to focus on anything and be productive when your physical environment and your mind are filled with clutter. If any of the above rings true for you, you'll be interested in learning five simple organizing concepts to create a productive environment. These concepts were articulated in 2003 by Barbara Hemphill in her book, *Love It or Lose It: Living Clutter-Free Forever,* published by BCI Press. They can apply to any environment or process.

Have a pencil and paper ready. Each step has important questions designed to make the overall process easier and more focused.

1. Design Your Vision

What do you want to organize or accomplish? Is it a room, your desk, your kitchen, your schoolwork, getting through your email or something else? What do you want it to look like? What will make you feel productive? Write down your vision or draw it out on paper or the computer. What will it feel like if it is organized? List your goals. Be specific. Without goals, how will you know that you have achieved your vision? For more on developing your vision, see Rhonda Elliott's chapter on *Capturing the Vision* on page 1.

I worked with a client who had a family room that had become her office, his office, the TV area, the exercise room, the clothes hanging room and a junk room. This client was overwhelmed by the space and needed to figure out what she really wanted this room to be now that the kids had grown up and moved out of the house. She knew she wanted space to do her research, pay her bills and email friends, as well as an open space to do her exercises. She also knew that she wanted her husband's office moved into one of the empty bedrooms. Ultimately, she decided that she wanted a desk area that gave her space for her computer and her genealogy research with a separate desk for her journaling and handwriting work. She wanted to use the exercise equipment while she watched TV. We drew the room with her activity areas in the appropriate dimensions so she could envision the new space. She was able to see her vision and make corrections as needed. She was ecstatic. She now has a place of her own to work productively, exercise and relax.

2. Eliminate Your Obstacles or Excuses

What isn't working? What's holding you back? Are you a pro-crastinator? What are the stumbling blocks you currently experience? Analyze your needs. What is working in the setup that you have? What have you tried in the past that didn't work? What is stopping your success?

A client recently purchased a business and was struggling with all the paperwork, the mail and the employees. He was great at sales on the phone but couldn't keep track of the orders he sold. As a new owner, he felt he needed to see and approve everything so it was all getting bottlenecked on his desk. We discussed his vision for a smooth and productive operation in his office. We discovered that there were procedures that the employees were not following, so we held a refresher-training course and got each of the three employees back on track. My client determined that he was able to delegate to one of the long-time employees and the flow of the orders in the office smoothed out. He also discovered that he now had more focused time to take the continuing education classes he needed to stay on top of his industry.

Take this same principle and apply it to your closet, kitchen or time. What's not working anymore? You can't find the gray sweater vest or the mate to the shoe in your hand. You are spending all your time looking for something rather than using it. Arrange your closet so all your sweaters are together in drawers, get a shoe rack for the door or the floor and use it all the time. Design the system to your specifications and then use it. Take a moment and think about your life. Are there any obstacles or excuses you need to eliminate?

For more information on creating an organized kitchen and closet, see Tina Oscar's chapter on *Conquering Kitchen Chaos,* page 83 and Toni Ahlgren's chapter on *Building Your Perfect Closet* on page 93, as well as Gretchen Ditto's *Wardrobe and Closet Bliss,* on page 105.

"Productivity is never an accident. It is always the result of a commitment to excellence, intelligent planning and focused effort."
—Paul J. Meyer, Founder, Success Motivation International Inc.

3. Commit Your Resources

What resources are you willing to invest in the project? Examples of resources include budget (money), time, technology and people. Basically, this means *you*. You are committing to invest your time and money, learn some new habits and practice and maintain those habits. Total up how much your lack of productivity may be costing in money, space, time and energy as we discussed in the first part of this chapter.

If you want to become more organized and productive, start small. You need to identify the first habit you want to change, start today and stay focused and consistent. Think through some other options and resources that perhaps you haven't considered up to this point.

One of the organizing processes that many of my clients adopt eagerly is that of organizing numerically rather than by subject or alphabetically. Organizing by numbers and keywords and then using a computerized database to help you locate the file, item or data you need is a different way of thinking about organizing. Filing or putting things back becomes very easy since you are simply filing numerically. You can use this process for CDs, videos, DVDs, books, collections and just about anything that you can number and describe. Using the computer makes finding what you are looking for very quick and productive. To what resources should you commit your productivity?

4. Select Your Tools

Based on your vision, obstacles and available resources, develop a plan of action tailored to your situation. Several general organizing concepts or methodologies will help you figure out a plan of action and the tools you need to create a more productive environment. Whether the issue is productivity in your kitchen, bathroom, garage, office or with your time, ask, "What will I do?" not "What should I do?" We tend to shy away from doing "shoulds." Here are some crucial tips:

Create a SYSTEM. SYSTEM stands for **S**ave **Y**ou **S**pace, **T**ime, **E**nergy, and **M**oney. What works for one person to save space, time, energy and money may or may not work for another. Some people need to have everything out in plain sight so they don't forget. Others make piles and some can put items out of sight with a reference to where those items are located. There is no right way to organize. You have to find the one that helps you create your productive environment and then maintain it.

Make sure everything has a place. You simply have to figure out what that place is for you. When you work or play, you want the things you use frequently nearby, within an arm's reach.

A client with a home-based business had turned her dining room into her office. She works in the real estate world and needed a great deal of reference material. She felt overwhelmed and knew that she was terribly disorganized and, as a result, very unproductive. She had a desk with a credenza and overhead shelving that she wasn't utilizing except to collect her items to file, her mail, her magazines and anything else with which she didn't know what to do. She housed the books she needed regularly in a shelving unit five feet away, so she continuously had to get up to get them. Then she would just leave them open on her desk and lay her work on top of them. When she needed the book again, she couldn't find it. It was buried beneath her paperwork, so she wasted time and energy running to the shelf looking for it, in vain.

We unloaded the shelves in her overhead shelving and housed the reference books there—permanently. Now whenever she needs to access one of those reference books, she reaches up from her seat, without standing, gets it down, uses it, and returns it to the overhead shelf when she is finished. She told me later that this one small change made such a positive difference in her productivity for her clients. I recommend that you figure out what you need where and put it there.

Eliminate emails. Begin working on the newest items first. For instance, if you are organizing your personal or business email, start with today's email first. If you begin with your oldest email, you will become tired, overwhelmed by the volume, distracted and quit. You won't be productive and will be haunted by a feeling of failure. Start with today's email. You can move all the older email into a folder called "Email Before [Date]." Then, take 15-20 minutes each day to organize, delete and so on some of that older email. You will have a feeling of accomplishment each day. You are staying on top of your current email and being productive.

Clear clutter with decisions. The items lying around our workspace, home, car or kitchen and even some activities in our life can often be classified as clutter if we no longer need them. They are there because no decision has been made about where they should be housed, filed or discarded.

As adults, we acquire clutter and allow it to get out of control because we aren't willing to make decisions about it. If you want to have a productive environment, you must make one of three decisions. The decisions are to File, Act or Toss (FAT).

- **File.** This is for the items or information you need to keep for reference or use. Following the Pareto Principle (the 80/20 rule,) we will only refer back to or use 20 percent of what we keep. Only file that 20 percent. Look at your closet. You really only wear 20 percent of the clothes hanging in it, right?

- **Act.** When the ball is in your court, you have a responsibility to take some action. Is it something that you need to do, go to, put into your calendar or delegate to someone else? Or someone you have to call or email? Follow the process you set up for each action.

- **Toss.** When you don't need it, eliminate it. Toss means many things—recycle, donate, delete and so on.

Become friendly with your wastebasket. What should I toss, recycle or get rid of? How do you make that decision? You can ask yourself the following questions:

- **Does this require a specific action or have a specific use?** If yes, then put it in your location for items to act on or where you will find it and use it. If no, then go to the next question.

- **Is it difficult to obtain again?** Be realistic here. If you will have a tough time getting the item or information again, then by all means, put it where you will find it again. If no, then go to the next question.

- **Is it recent enough to be useful?** Much of the information or items you keep are no longer up to date—old computers, printers, documents, magazines, clothing and so on. Another way to apply this question is to see if you've worn it, used it or fixed it in the last year. If the answer is yes, then keep it. Otherwise, go to the next question.

- **Are there tax or legal implications?** Usually, this question refers to documentation of any action you have taken. There are specific retention periods for many documents, particularly if you are a business owner. Check with your tax accountant and attorney. See www.keckler.com/recordretention.htm for both business and personal record retention guidelines.

- **What's the worst thing that could happen without it?** If you can live with the results of not having the item or document, then toss, recycle or donate it. If you must keep it, then do so and put it into your retrieval system so you can easily locate it when necessary.

5. Maintain Your Success

To have a productive environment over time, you must implement your plan of action, take that first action and then include a method or system for maintaining the plan. Does the system or process work? Do you like it? Are you seeing positive consequences? If you answer no to any of these questions, go through the first four steps again and see what needs to be changed.

Creating a productive environment requires knowing what you need to design and accomplish your vision and then determining your obstacles and overcoming them. Consider your energy, time, money and space while selecting your tools. Implement a plan to accomplish your vision, and then follow through to maintain your goal.

You will find every step you make toward being organized increases your ability to be productive, de-stressed and successful. Work toward your goals from an environment that supports you and who you want to be.

SANDY STELTER, JD, CPO®
SOS – Strategic Organizing Solutions

(707) 425-4767
sandy@sos2day.com
www.sos2day.com

Working smarter, not harder, is the goal for people in every walk of life. We all know how to work hard, but with the myriad of activities in our lives, we aren't as productive as we would like. Since 1994, Sandy has worked with hundreds of clients to help them get rid of the pain and learn how to create and maintain a productive environment anywhere.

Sandy Stelter, owner of SOS – Strategic Organizing Solutions, holds a BA in Library Science and a JD. She spent five years of her corporate career in Records Management as an analyst responsible for creating filing systems and retention programs. She spent another 12 years managing a software-testing department for a legal publisher. SOS began as a natural outgrowth of Sandy's organizing and management skills with an emphasis on efficiency and productivity, yielding more time for other areas of her clients' lives.

SOS provides consultation and hands-on professional, customized, productivity coaching to individuals and businesses. Sandy is the current Treasurer of the National Association of Professional Organizers (NAPO) and an active member of her local Chambers of Commerce.

Organizing for
High **Performance** Families
By Anna Sicalides, CPO®

*"Time is the coin of your life. It is the only coin you have and only
you can determine how it will be spent. Be careful,
lest you let other people spend it for you."*
—Carl Sandburg, American poet, writer and editor

You may find you are living your life flying by the seat of your pants.
You have no time for yourself or your family. You are having 16 people
for dinner this weekend and you have no menu planned. You have no
idea what your kids' schedules are or what country your spouse will be
in next week. There is a nagging in the back of your mind that you are
forgetting something, only to realize later that you have missed an
important meeting. Do you ever feel like your life is a runaway train?

This is not uncommon among high performance families. In order to
create a life that is more productive and rewarding, you need to
reevaluate how you do things. This chapter will provide you with
fundamental tools that you can use to create the life you deserve.

*"Insanity: Doing the same thing over and over again and expecting
different results."*
—Albert Einstein, German-American physicist, Nobel Prize winner

High Performance Defined

High performance families are goal-oriented, driven to achieve at a higher level and always looking for ways to make improvements. These families carry a lot of responsibility through their families, their jobs, their volunteer and charitable works and other involvements. The children in these families are also high achievers, with heavy workloads in school and many extracurricular activities. Personal and family time for high performance families is in short supply. They never have enough hours in the day and have high stress levels. It is time to stop that runaway train!

Big Picture Thinking

Try to think of the big picture, not the task right in front of you. Through horseback riding lessons, I learned to look ahead and when you need to, turn your head in the direction you want to go and the horse will go there as well. It's amazing. This same thing applies to organizing your life. Don't worry at first about what tasks are directly in front of you; think about what you want your life to look like. Once you do this, you will be able to fill in the steps that will get you there.

The more crowded your calendar, the harder it is to slow down long enough to see the big picture and do the necessary planning. Find some time in between your commitments, perhaps while waiting for someone or, better yet, arrange to get away from it all for an hour or two. Sit down and make two lists: (1) what you want your life to look like and (2) how you want your family to work. These lists will become your guide.

Remember that making life changes is part of a process and can take time. It's like taking the local train rather than the express. It is important to enjoy the ride!

High Expectations

"I am careful not to confuse excellence with perfection.
Excellence, I can reach for; perfection is God's business."
—Michael J. Fox, Canadian actor, author, advocate

High performance individuals put a lot of pressure on themselves and those around them. High expectations are great but unreasonable expectations are dangerous. I encourage my clients to realize when something is "good enough." This takes some practice, yet it is possible to change this thinking. Let's look at striving for excellence and achievement rather than perfection.

I worked with a client who was a lifelong perfectionist. As we were working together, I asked her what "good enough" was to her. She started to realize that "good enough" was actually completely acceptable in many cases and with this realization she was able to move through her projects much more quickly. Embracing "good enough" and turning down the volume of her perfectionism also supported her in becoming involved in a new and healthy relationship.

Boundaries

Boundaries can be an issue for high performing individuals and families. The desire to please and get positive recognition is very enticing. If you are overcommitted, I recommend that you take time throughout your day to pause and reflect. Ask yourself questions like, "Will this commitment come at the cost of something else and is that okay with me?" or "Does accepting this commitment fit in with my value system and vision for my life and my family?" Be selective with your choices. You only want to add value and that which will help you achieve your vision. It is wise for high performance individuals to learn to say "No" and trust that another opportunity will usually come around. I truly believe that when one door closes, another will open and you can decide if that is the door you want to walk through.

I worked with a client who was overcommitted and unhappy about much of the board and committee responsibilities she had taken on. I asked her what her dreams and passions were. She realized that she really wanted to write a book to help adolescents live through tragic situations. She has stepped down from many of her board and committee responsibilities elsewhere and now actively researches this topic and involves herself with organizations that work with this issue. It is wonderful to see her having a focus and purpose that has given her life much more meaning. She is truly a happier human being.

Managing Your High Performance Family

Think of your family responsibilities in the same way you do your work. Running your family is like running a corporation. One of my clients considers herself the CEO of her household. She is the go-to person for almost everything organizational, physical and emotional that goes on in her household.

Management is the skill of planning, organizing, leading and directing to accomplish the vision that you and your family want. We are all responsible for managing ourselves, our family, our homes and our time.

Here are some tools and tips to better manage:

Binders. This is an important tool if you like paper and it goes everywhere with you. Think of having all the information you need on a daily or weekly basis at your fingertips. Use plastic sleeves and tabs or hole punch the sheets to create sections, either by person or activity or sometimes both. Contact lists, calendars, sports schedules, meal plans and business cards go into this binder. Buy yourself a binder that you love. Pick the color and style that inspire you. If it doesn't have a design, feel free to add your own.

Technology. I am a fan of technology. It can save a lot of time, although I am aware and know from experience that it can become a time waster if you are not careful. If you do use technology, here are a few important timesavers:

- **Online banking.** It's faster and cheaper and you don't need envelopes, checks or stamps. If you keep plenty of cash in your checking account, then an even easier step is to use automatic bill payments. No matter which method you choose, you must check your statements regularly to verify their accuracy. One of my clients who was initially quite resistant to this was thrilled to discover how she could sit at her desk and pay all of her bills in such a short amount of time. This enabled her to minimize late payments and interest charges, as well as improve her credit scores.

- **Online grocery ordering.** Did you know that many grocery stores offer online ordering? Although some charge a small fee plus a tip for this service, you are likely to save a lot of money by eliminating impulse purchasing. And the time you save should well cover the minimal fee. Some services store your history online so you can use your history to place new orders and most deliver right to your kitchen.

- **Three-way calling.** This is one of the most underused features on our phones. Using three-way calling can save a lot of time when making plans or getting a consensus. My sisters and I used this when we were settling a relative's estate. We were able to get together on a call, discuss issues with the estate sale company and make decisions. This kept the project moving forward easily and effortlessly.

- **Smart phones.** Using the calendar, contact and notes features of smart phones alone will make a difference. Since you can simply toss the phone in your pocket or purse, it is always with you, as opposed to planners that are less portable.

  I had two clients who were constantly missing appointments and running around frazzled. They both purchased smart phones and it made an amazing difference.

Planning Meals

There are many ways to plan meals. Some people have great success with charts or index cards—menu on front, ingredients on back. You can create any number of weeks of the meals that your family enjoys. For example, you can have turkey Mondays, ground beef on Tuesdays, chicken on Wednesdays, beans and rice on Thursdays and seafood on Fridays. Then you can rotate these if you'd like. Even if you stick to it 60 percent of the time, you come out ahead. For more in-depth information on meal planning, see Tina Oscar's chapter on *Conquering Kitchen Chaos* on page 83.

Delegation

Delegating means giving someone a task. Use any resources you may have—your kids, your spouse, willing friends and family members, your peers, people on your teams and committees and of course those that you pay to do things. Use your time for what you do best. You wouldn't put a new roof on your house yourself, would you?

The key to successful delegation is to give the appropriate task to the appropriate person. Give that person your clear intention, instructions and an agreed-upon deadline and then verify that the individual understands the task. If someone is doing something new or challenging, check in periodically to make sure he or she is on track.

Also remember that once you teach someone to do a task for you that person will be able to do it for you repeatedly. The investment you make will pay off in time. Remember to show your gratitude and appreciation for work well done.

A common roadblock to being a good delegator is that you feel you are the only person who can do the job or do it fast enough. Therefore, you don't ask. You may feel you should do it yourself because you think asking for help is a sign of weakness or failure. I remind you to adopt the frame of mind that most things just need to be done "well enough," not perfectly.

Some people to whom you can delegate are:

- **Virtual assistants.** They can schedule appointments, make follow-up phone calls, do phone or Internet research, create invitations, plan events, pay bills and much more, depending on your needs and your VA's services.

- **Personal chefs.** They can purchase food, cook, clean up and freeze your meals. Most can accommodate a variety of dietary needs.

- **Bookkeepers.** They can pay your bills, track your investments and expenses and generate reports as you need them. This is a lifesaver for tax preparation.

- **Personal shoppers.** They can shop for you. They will come to your house and assess what you have and what you need and then make purchases for you. Also, using their services for gift purchases is a real time saver. One client has her personal shopper put together five outfits every season, then she fills in casual, workout and evening wear as needed. This is a huge time saver for her.

- **Personal trainers, yoga and Pilates instructors.** They will come to your house and bring basic items with them. You can get your workout at your convenience. What a great way to start the day.

- **Family members.** Each family member can bear some responsibility for how the home and their lives are run. Engaging everyone in daily and weekly tasks helps the home manager and teaches the other members of the team to take responsibility.

One family with whom I have worked had general clutter around their house. I suggested that the family get together for 10-15 minutes every day they were home and have a family pick-up time. Every time I went back to their house, it looked better. It helped them to set a timer each time. They were actually having fun and the kids were learning how to pick up after themselves.

Another client has several college interns helping at her house. I was there one day prior to a party and she had a task list for each intern and outside contractor. She gave each one a brief overview and let them get to work on their assignments. While we were working on paper management, she was getting amazing amounts of other work done throughout her home.

Keep the idea of delegation in the front of your mind. More ideas for service providers will come to you as you adapt to doing things differently.

Scheduling

There seem to be two types of people—the technologically-oriented and the paper-oriented. My clients who have changed from paper calendars to technology-oriented calendars have greatly improved their time management. You have to make that choice. Remember, you can always switch back or make changes.

Schedule the things you need to stick to or the things that really matter to you. I suggest you purchase a simple, old-fashioned timer—the kind that ticks. Set your timer for the amount of time you want to commit to a certain task. I have a client who schedules all repairmen to come to her house on Mondays—the day she and I work together. This way, she is available when they need her and she is also moving ahead in her organizing.

I highly recommend consolidating everyone's schedules into one location. Google Calendar is a great, free, online resource. Everyone in your family can enter his or her schedule there. Your password-protected calendar can then be accessed from anywhere with an Internet connection.

Time to Get Started

It is time to get on the train! Realize the big picture and reframe your high expectations. Set clear boundaries and continue thinking of how you can pass some responsibility on to others. This will give you more time to review your schedule and plan.

I have passed a lot of information on to you that will help you take the necessary steps to organize your high performance family. The ideas are endless. Be creative. Add some of your own ideas to this list. Once you start to implement some of these strategies, you will see a great difference in your life. The train is pulling into the station with you on it. Enjoy the journey!

ANNA SICALIDES, CPO®
The Organizing Consultant

Chaos eradicated! Aggravation abolished!
Overwhelm obliterated!

(484) 432-8692
anna@annaorganizesu.com
www.annaorganizesu.com

The Organizing Consultant, LLC, located on Philadelphia's Main Line, was founded by Anna Sicalides, CPO® in 2002. Anna's expertise is working with high performance families, individuals undergoing life transitions, and individuals committed to minimizing their organizational stress. Her clients range from the families of CEOs running global businesses to busy, overwhelmed families, to someone who has suffered a personal loss.

Anna works with her clients to define what truly brings value to their lives and focuses on creating environments, solutions and systems to nurture their goals and vision. Anna's experience as a retail executive working with space challenges, staff training, high level customer service skills and her constant thirst for education have given her the tools to guide her clients to success. Her biggest thrill is to help people and watch their lives transform through their work together.

Recognized as a leader in her field, Anna has served on the board of the Philadelphia chapter of the National Association of Professional Organizers (NAPO) since 2003, with three terms as President. She currently co-chairs the Chapter Relations Committee of NAPO. Anna has been featured in *The Philadelphia Inquirer* and several local publications.

Win at Organizing
Overcoming Chronic Disorganization

By Anne Blumer, CPO®

We all encounter situations in our lives when we become disorganized. You might experience a move or you might take on a new job that requires more of your time. You or someone close to you may become ill and you can no longer keep up with your day-to-day activities. Perhaps you recently lost your job or lost a loved one. This is called "situational" disorganization and it is an understandable and normal part of life.

Chronic disorganization happens when these events occur and you do not quickly or easily return to a state of organization. Instead, the disorganization does not improve and may even continue to worsen over time. At some point, your day-to-day activities become so overwhelming and stressful that you need help to restore order. If your quality of life is suffering, you feel stressed and overwhelmed much of the time and you do not feel like you can correct the course yourself, you may be "chronically" disorganized.

Chronic disorganization is a term coined by Judith Kolberg in her book, *Conquering Chronic Disorganization,* published in 1999 by Squall Press. Judith defines chronic disorganization as disorganization that has a long history, undermines one's quality of life on a daily basis and recurs.

Some Causes of Chronic Disorganization

Chronic disorganization is *not* a medical issue. However, chronic disorganization is commonly associated with other medical issues such as Attention Deficit Disorder (ADD), chronic pain, depression, bi-polar disorder, Alzheimer's, brain injury and autistic spectrum disorders. It can also be associated with a compulsion or addiction to shopping or acquiring things beyond a reasonable amount.

How to Tell if You Are Chronically Disorganized

If you answer yes to any of the questions below, you could be chronically disorganized:

- Has disorganization been a factor in your life for many years?
- Does your level of disorganization interfere with your quality of life or negatively impact your relationship with others?
- Does your disorganization persist despite self-help efforts such as reading books on organization or purchasing organizing containers?
- Are you embarrassed by your clutter and do not invite people over?
- Are you easily distracted and find it difficult to focus?
- Do you feel there is something wrong with you because you have tried to get organized before and you keep slipping back to a state of disorganization?

How to Win at Organizing and Overcome Chronic Disorganization

Most people are able to get organized and maintain organization using conventional methods, such as a filing system, that has a logical method to filing and retrieving information. However, chronically disorganized individuals are not conventional and are more emotional-based versus logic-based when it comes to organizing.

Let's look at ways to overcome chronic disorganization, organizing criteria that will help you decide what to keep and what to let go of, how to break through emotional-based organizing stumbling blocks and how to create new habits to sustain organization that will help you win at organizing.

Where to Start

Sometimes just knowing how to stop cluttering and where to start organizing is the most daunting part of the organization process, especially for the chronically disorganized and individuals with ADD. Here are a few rules of thumb to follow when you head down your path to a more organized and clutter-free life.

1. Create your vision. This is the first step in the organizing process for any project. Use a spiral notebook to capture thoughts, ideas and solutions for each room in your home. Some questions to ask yourself are:

- What is the purpose of this space?
- What activities will take place in this space?
- Do I have all of the items I need to support those activities?
- What are my current habits with this space?
- What is my vision for how the space will look, feel and function?

For more on creating your vision see Rhonda Elliott's chapter on *Capturing the Vision* on page 1.

2. Begin with your biggest frustration. Ask yourself, "What is causing me the most frequent frustration?" Is it that pile of paper on top of your kitchen counter? Is it your kitchen pantry? Is it never finding your keys as you start to head out the door each day? Is it your child's, once again, late homework project?

3. Plan your attack. Plan time for your organizing project. Four-hour blocks work best. Have the materials and resources you need on hand (garbage bags, drop box, stickers/labels to identify where items will go and boxes for sorting). Do not buy containers until you have sorted and purged your items to know how many you need. Arrange with the charity of your choice to pick up your items for donation immediately after you have completed your organizing project.

4. Work with others. If you are chronically disorganized or have ADD, you can benefit greatly from working with someone to help you stay focused. This also makes the process more energizing and fun. Sometimes you may just need another person with you acting as a "body double." According to Judith Kolberg, a body double's principal job is to occupy space while you do organizing chores. He or she must be quiet and non-distracting, nonjudgmental, patient and able to sit still for long periods of time without touching anything.

Tips for Chronically Disorganized People and Individuals with ADD

- Find a quiet place to work or study so you are not distracted by sounds or by others.

- Set time limits. Timers will help you stay on schedule and focused.

- Create visuals. Calendars, wipe-and-write boards, Post-it® notes or pictures are a few visuals that create great reminders.

- Delegate the things you do not like doing or are not good at doing to someone else. Hire a housekeeper, a coach, an accountant or an assistant to help you.

- Break up the task into smaller parts if you find large tasks overwhelming. This makes them more manageable and achievable.

- Ask questions out loud. Hearing what you need to do can move the decision-making process along.
- Do one task at a time, such as collecting trash from all over the house at the same time or putting all dishes in the dishwasher at one time.

Deciding What to Keep and What to Let Go Of

Realize that organizing is not an overnight process and you are often faced with difficult decisions about what to keep and what to let go of. The first step is *deciding what is important to you today.*

Here are some "keep or let go of" criteria questions to help aid you through the decision-making process and help you clarify what is important and what is no longer important to you.

For every "No" answer, consider tossing the item.

- Is it useful and beautiful to you?
- If you keep it, will you remember you have it?
- Will you display it or use it?
- Do you need it?
- Have you used this item in the past six months?
- Is this adding value to your life today?
- Is it irreplaceable?
- Are you realistically going to finish this quilt (or other project)?
- Does it make you happy to see it?
- Do you love it?
- Are you honoring and enjoying it?
- Does it lift your spirits to look at it?

- Are you legally required to keep it?
- Is there a tax reason to keep it?

For every "Yes" answer, consider tossing the item.

- If you took a picture of it, would that make it easier for you to let it go?
- Are you keeping it because someone gave it to you and you will feel guilty if you let go of it?
- Does it make you mad, sad or feel bad to see it?
- Do you have anything else that reminds you of this event, person or time?
- Are you putting things before people and relationships?
- Is it a duplicate?
- Is it too worn/broken/unidentifiable?

Stumbling Blocks

Often during the deciding part of the organizing process, you may make excuses for not letting go of an item or what I call stumbling blocks. Here are six of the more common stumbling blocks and my responses to help you see a more realistic perspective.

1. *I might need it someday.* For each item you think you need to keep because it might be useful someday, look at it as though you were packing it for a move. Ask yourself these questions, "Does the item still have a purpose in my life today?" "If I were to keep this item, where would it live in my home?" "Why is it not living there in my current home?" If you still believe you cannot let go of the item because you think you will need it someday, then place it in a box and circle a day on your calendar as "someday." If you have not used the items by that date, then toss them. Hanging on to stuff you are not currently using makes it harder to access the things you are using.

2. *I don't know which papers to keep.* The amount of paperwork you receive can cause you to freeze, especially when much of it seems to be important. Essentially, you keep the paperwork for which there is purpose. Here are five purposeful papers to keep:

- Taxes
- Resale of property/cost basis
- Agreements
- Certificates/legal proof
- Returns (receipts) or disputes (claims)

Be clear what the purpose is and store the paper so that you can access it when you need it.

3. *It was a gift.* Once a gift is given to you, you are free to do with it what you choose. The object is not the gift. It is the act of giving that is the gift. Someone thought of you and wanted to express their thoughts in a tangible way. I'm sure you never gave anyone a gift and thought, "I love you very much and I hope this is a burden to you for the rest of your life!" The love is in the giving. Use it and love it or give it to someone who can. You have my permission to get rid of any gift you do not use or love.

4. *It reminds me of my mother.* You may associate an object with a special memory of someone. But the memory is actually inside of you, not outside. You can choose to take a picture and let go of the object. Or to preserve the memory, you can write about it in a journal and even place the picture of the item with your journal entry. There it will be preserved so that you will not forget and generations after you will have the memory as well.

5. *I paid a lot of money for it.* The monetary value of any item is only that for which you could sell it. Do not hesitate to part with something simply because you paid a lot of money for it. Keeping items that do not serve a purpose in your life today costs you in terms of lost productivity and sacrifice of freedom. Plus, it is often a negative energy. Perhaps it makes you angry that you spent a lot of money for something that you are not using any more and keeping that item around is a constant reminder of your anger. In addition, if you are storing items in an offsite storage unit, consider the cost savings without it.

6. *I don't have the time to get organized.* Your free time is very precious and the last thing you want to do is spend it eliminating the clutter in your life. However, clutter is overtaking your time already. Consider the time, energy and effort that are sapped from you mentally and psychologically with the clutter you have now in your life. You have to spend all your energy just coping with the mess, rather than tending to the things that really matter to you. No matter how deep the clutter is, you can make the time to free yourself from it.

How to Stay Organized

You will win at organizing if you follow these ten organizing habits and incorporate them into your maintenance plans where suitable:

1. One in—one out. When something new comes into your home, make it a rule that something must leave.

2. Before you buy. Before you buy an item, decide where it will live in your home. If you do not know, do not buy. Also, consider if you really need the item.

3. Containers. Buy containers only when you know what will go in them. Containers are often purchased to solve an organizing problem only to create more clutter because you do not know what to do with them or where to place them.

4. Label everything. By labeling, you will know where to put things away and more importantly, others with whom you share your home will know where to put them away. A label can be words, pictures or a combination of both.

5. Don't zigzag. Choose an area to organize and stick with that area. If you find something that belongs in another area of your home, do not move it until you are finished organizing the space you started in.

6. Prioritize. Keeping everything makes nothing important. Decide what is truly important in your life and that will help you focus on what to keep and honor.

7. Be decisive. Clutter is caused by deferred decisions. Do not wait to make a decision about where something belongs; decide immediately and put it there. Return it to its home whenever it wanders away.

8. Set a limit. Set a limit on how many of something you are going to keep—for example, magazines. Decide to keep one year's worth of each subscription and recycle the rest. Also, set a limit on the amount of space you are allocating to a collection, such as one shelf.

9. Paper. Ask yourself, "Can I get this information somewhere else, such as the Internet or the library?" If you can easily access the information somewhere else, then toss it. You will actually refer to only 20 percent of what you file for reference.

10. Maintenance. Organizing is not a one-time "clean sweep" event. Create and follow a maintenance plan for all the areas in your life and home. You can do all the grouping, reducing and organizing you want, but if you do not learn the skills and follow a plan, you will backslide. A maintenance plan will reinforce new habits and eventually replace the old habits that have been keeping you disorganized. A *simple* maintenance plan addresses *what* is required to be done and at what *frequency*, such as daily, weekly, monthly and so on.

I encourage you to choose one small area to de-clutter and organize. It could be something such as a work surface, drawer, cabinet or box. Apply the techniques and tips offered in this chapter. Create new habits and behaviors to support maintenance of this one small area and then move on to another area. You can win at organizing! Enjoy your success.

ANNE BLUMER, CPO®
SolutionsForYou, Inc.

*Providing effortless solutions
to organizing*

(503) 246-0710
anne@solutionsforyou.com
www.solutionsforyou.com

Founder of SolutionsForYou, Inc., Anne offers professional organizing services to corporate, residential and SOHO clients. Through the Professional Organizer Training Institute,™ Anne has trained hundreds of professional organizers how to launch, manage and grow profitable businesses. The institute was nominated for the 2010 NAPO LA Organizing Awards Most Valuable Educational Resource.

With her years of managerial experience, Anne understands the organizational skills needed to be a professional in today's competitive business place. As a mother, she also knows firsthand what it takes to organize a busy family and keep a household running smoothly. Anne teaches her clients how to achieve work-life balance through organization, habits and routines.

Anne is a Certified Professional Organizer.® Additionally, she holds a certificate of training from the Coach Approach for Organizers™ and the National Study Group on Chronic Disorganization (NSGCD), a Level II ADD Specialist certificate and Level II Chronic Disorganization Specialist certificate. Anne is a Golden Circle member of NAPO, NAPO Oregon and the NSGCD. She is the recipient of NAPO Oregon's 2009 President's Award. She has a bachelor's degree in Organizational Communication from Maryhurst University in Oregon. Anne is the author of *Get Rich Organizing*.

How to **Choose** Your Professional Organizer
By Natasha Packer

Before you can get organized, you need to know who is going to help you! In this chapter, I will lead you through the process to determine the perfect match for you according to the job you need to get done. Whether it is information or spatial organizing, time management or systems consulting, partnering with the right professional organizer facilitates your project satisfaction. The clients of professional organizers vary as much as the Seattle weather. The right professional organizer will help you discover what you need if you are not certain or if you are certain, and how best to achieve the results you want.

The National Association of Professional Organizers points out that a successful professional organizer has the ability to "ask the right questions, teach and transfer basic skills, use technology to support your efforts, listen and infer what a client means and break goals down into manageable steps." Besides all this, they champion, motivate, propel and spearhead projects. Throughout this chapter, wherever you see the word *organizer,* know that I mean your "professional organizer," not an agenda, scheduler or other product.

Searching for the Right Organizer

Here are four things for which to look when you are finding the right organizer for you.

1. Good rapport and communication. Communication empowers the relationship. Every facet of your working relationship is enhanced by open and honest communication. Look for someone with whom you can develop a good rapport and with whom you feel comfortable sharing why you want to be organized. Sometimes, organizing can get emotional and overwhelming. Working with someone with whom you can share your feelings along the way and who will respect your feelings is essential to your organizing success.

2. In alignment with your needs. Professional organizers have a variety of skills and knowledge to assist their clients. You may be looking for assistance from someone with a fresh perspective on relocating, or someone experienced at estate management or someone to advise you how to stay organized for your first career. Some organizers are individuals while others are teams devoted to specialties. Whatever your special organizing need is, there is an organizer out there who can help you meet your objectives.

3. Know-how and skills. The level of experience and abilities you will find in an organizer will vary. The project dictates your choice of organizer. Professional organizers have a wide variety of backgrounds. Some organizers will have a corporate background with years of experience while others have chosen this profession as their first career. Both types could be advantageous. Your organizer will present suggestions, ideas and thoughts to bring you into organizing reality. Of course this does not mean that person will ignore your preferences.

However, there will be times that your organizer will be better informed regarding the best solution and it is their responsibility to help you achieve success.

4. In your price range. Hiring an organizer is an investment and should be seen as a value-added service. Part of searching for an organizer is choosing one that you can afford. But how do you determine your investment for your project? Some organizers work on a project basis, others by the hour. Always discuss up front the projected costs of your project with your organizer. Get all estimates and costs in writing before you begin.

There are thousands of professional organizers in North America and many may be located in your area. The National Association of Professional Organizers allows you to do a search for an organizer close to you (www.napo.net.) Be sure to visit their websites before you call to make sure their specialties match the scope of your project.

"You must do the thing you think you cannot do."
—Eleanor Roosevelt, humanitarian and civil rights advocate

Plan Ahead for the Project

There is no exact picture of disorganization. You don't have to be a hoarder to hire an organizer. Those who need a professional organizer in their business range from the one-person/home-based business to the micro-business; from the direct sales representative to the large 500+ employee company. You may hire an organizer for space management, event organizing, time management, office management or training of employees.

Your needs may require a range of solutions from simple office assistance, system setup, electronic filing and management counseling, to workshops for your employees. Many organizers have the experience level you are looking for and can offer many solutions to your everyday processes. Your search for the organizer appropriate to your needs could require interviewing a handful of professionals before deciding on one. Depending on the size of your business, you may choose to hire a team of professionals instead of one individual. Regardless, they are ready to do great things for your company and can be a cost-effective solution, perhaps better than hiring full-time staff or using your current staff's time.

For an individual or family with organizing needs, your solutions will range from simple product solutions to re-designing a space, from recycling to purging extensively. With this in mind, look for the organizer who will listen, push and encourage you. Keep in mind that you might want to tell stories and share, so the organizer's patience and a good sense of humor are indispensable. For the right organizer, you will be an enjoyable experience for them, not a burden.

Before you go looking for the right organizer for you, there are some questions to answer about yourself. Once you answer the questions below, it is time to make an assessment appointment.

- What is it I want organized?
- Am I ready to get rid of some of my stuff?
- Do I want a team of organizers or just one?
- In what do I need the professional organizer or company to specialize, in order to meet my needs?

Building Trust

Let's assume you are ready to hire your organizer. Your relationship will begin with a phone call or email. You will both be getting to know each other. Do not hesitate to ask for referrals and get them before you book an assessment appointment.

Build a relationship based on trust, and together you will collaborate on the best path to accomplish your project. You will share your vision and, based on his or her experience, knowledge and skill, your organizer will present solutions. Don't be afraid to ask any questions you need answered. Here are some questions to ask your prospective organizer:

- How long have you been in business?
- What kind of clients do you mostly serve and what do you do for them?
- What training or background do you have?
- Are you insured and bonded?
- What do you feel is your greatest strength as an organizer?
- Will you be the only one coming to assist me or will you send or bring someone else?
- (If needed) Do you provide ongoing organizing support?

Any professional organizer will easily answer your questions. Do not hesitate to interview a few people to find your best match. During the initial appointment you and the organizer will begin to solidify a strong relationship.

Your First Meeting

During the initial appointment, the organizer is evaluating the scope of the project and whether to accept you as a client while you are completing your evaluation of him or her.

He or she may make suggestions that at first appear to not be the perfect solution. I encourage you to be open to the possibility that there is more than one way to look at the project. For example, you may initially feel you know exactly how to get from point A to point B in your project and just want the organizer to follow instructions. As simple as this may seem, the high level of skill and knowledge you have purchased might dictate a new process of getting from point A to point B. The organizer always has your best interests in mind, and wants your project to be smooth and cost effective too.

If you determine that the relationship won't work, please kindly thank the person, pay the assessment fee and move on to the next organizer.

Key Steps to the Process

Your organizer will have four key steps to lead your project to success.

1. Correctly assess the scenario
2. Put together an organizing action plan
3. Transfer organizing skills
4. Maintain the project results

Let's take a look at each one:

1. Correctly assess the scenario. Before presenting a system, the organizer does an evaluation of the project and circumstances. How you are in your environment helps the organizer engineer a plan, discover what solutions you have used before, why they didn't work and conceptualize the future. This takes an enormous amount of skill, discernment and experience on the part of the organizer.

2. Put together an organizing action plan. Your organizer will ask you a series of questions. These questions will help your organizer determine the results you want and what processes may be needed to achieve your goals. By the end of the conversation your organizer will know exactly what your expectations are and the results you want.

3. Transfer organizing skills to you. During the project, you will learn the skill of how to organize. Whether it is re-arranging, sorting, discarding or replacing, you and your organizer will upgrade your environment. You will learn new skills and new habits will be formed. For example, in the past you might have thought spring-cleaning was something you do once a year. However, your organizer will help you understand why it is better to deep clean your home at least once each of the four seasons. By breaking the project down into manageable pieces, it doesn't overwhelm or feel like it will take forever, because it will be a lighter cleaning list each successive season after the initial cleaning session.

4. Maintain the beautiful project results. Once your project is complete you may want some support to maintain your organized environment. Some organizers provide ongoing maintenance. This can involve as little as follow-up calls or as much as regular successive appointments. Some clients choose to only organize their garage, for instance, and once it is accomplished they feel satisfied and can manage it well. Others have a space that runs rampant on a consistent basis. Discuss with your organizer how you are going to maintain the organized space. Regardless, your organizer will call every once in a while just to make sure everything is still going as smoothly as when he or she left. This is your opportunity to have him or her back and work with you on a new project as well. Through proper attention and guidance from your professional organizer you will enjoy a more organized home or business life.

Application

Take what you have read in this chapter and apply it now. Remember the four keys to choosing the right professional organizer are good communication, alignment with your needs, in your price range and a match of know-how and skills to accomplish your projects. Now you know how to work effectively with an organizer and how to assess who is the best match for you and your project. Go do it!

NATASHA PACKER
As You Wish

We empower organized homes
and businesses to run smoothly

(206) 459-2955
natasha@organizingasyouwish.com
www.organizingasyouwish.com

Natasha's business as a professional organizer focuses on home-based small businesses and individual homeowners who have an entrepreneurial spirit. She enjoys joining forces in localized presentations to improve business functionalities such as starting a small business, how to market it and dedicating time to growing the business. Coaching homeowners in time efficiency, smart storage solutions and unique solutions for each individual has been her key to success. As a strong believer in continuing education, she also continues to educate herself and her employees by constantly learning about new methods, products and styles. However, it is Natasha's relaxed and confident manner that leads clients to view her as the expert organizer she is.

Natasha naturally came to this profession through experience. She has mastered both the large and small office environment and rounded out her skills by gaining experience as a nanny, a team player in commercial construction and a public volunteer. She is a member of the National Association of Professional Organizers (NAPO) and the local Seattle Chapter. Having a good time and focusing her clients on how being organized can be fun has lead to her success.

Staging Your Home

Transforming Your Space to Eliminate Clutter and Fit Your Lifestyle

By Janet Schiesl

Have you ever walked into a room and immediately felt comfortable? Whether it was a friend's living room or a reception area in an office, attention to detail often sets the stage for a welcoming space. In this chapter, you will learn how to reorganize your space to work for your lifestyle. Unlike today's popular television shows that teach you how to stage your home for sale, you will explore ways to stage your home so you can keep clutter at bay and use your space to its greatest potential.

We will focus on five living spaces: living room, dining room, bedroom, home office and kitchen. You will see how the four elements of staging will enhance how you live in your home. The first element to consider in each space is a focal point. It is the feature to which your eyes are drawn when you enter a room. A focal point is what defines a room. Furniture placement is the second element on which you will work to revitalize your space. Next, we will focus on storage within each room. Adequate storage allows you to have a home for everything and not create incidental clutter. Lighting is the finishing touch when staging any space. With some experimentation, you will experience how lighting can change the mood in a room.

Staging each area of your home should take less than one day. Each project should cost you little, if anything. I will encourage you to reevaluate how you use each space in your home. To begin, you should simplify your space by eliminating items you do not use or love. But unlike the television shows, staging for your life does not mean depersonalizing your space. You do have to live there and in this process, you are the expert.

Room 1: The Living Room

"Without a TV, how would you know where to put the sofa?"
—An ABC Ad, 1998-99 TV campaign by TBWA

Architectural features such as a fireplace or a large picture window can be the focal point in your living room. If you do not have an architectural feature, your focal point may be a large piece of artwork or a piece of furniture like an armoire. Note that I said large. Think about what you want to communicate about your life. As pointed out in the quote above, for many of us, the focal point of the room where we spend a lot of our free time is a television. If that's okay with you, then it's okay with me. However, you may realize from doing this exercise that you no longer want the focal point of the main room in your home to be the television. This space is meant to meet your needs and work for you. Identify the focal point in your living room to start staging.

Furniture placement is the next task you need to explore in the staging process. Identify the largest piece of furniture in your living room. It is probably a sofa. It should be placed to face the room's focal point. Place other furniture like chairs, a coffee table and side tables within a ten-foot diameter circle to create a conversation area.

Great rooms in today's modern homes can create their own challenge by being so large that furniture placement becomes difficult. If your room is large, consider separating it into two conversation areas. Instead of pushing all the furniture up against the wall so the kids can

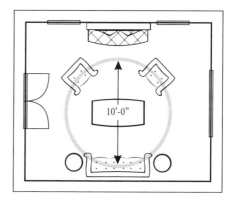

play in the middle of the room, break the room up by placing a conversation area at one end of the room. This will help define the spaces for different activities, like play and TV watching.

Everyone needs storage in every room of a home. Consider what activities you do in the living room and plan storage for each activity. If you enjoy sitting in one of your cozy chairs to read or knit, place a table or storage cabinet next to the chair. Also, place a bookcase nearby if you have a large collection waiting for your attention. Do you play games in this room? Locate space on a bookcase or in a nearby closet to store your games. This is where it becomes really important to give serious thought to what you need to keep and what should be located somewhere else in your home. Clutter will collect in areas where there is not enough storage for the things you do in the space. Relocate to another room anything that is not part of your regular living room activities.

The finishing touch in every room is lighting. It can set or change the mood in a room. In your living room, add a light source at every seat. Lighting can be in the form of ceiling, table or floor lamps and of course the natural light that comes from windows. Each type of lighting creates different effects in the room. Two pieces of furniture placed next to each other can share lighting.

Room 2: The Dining Room

The largest and most important piece of furniture in the dining room is the table. It is usually placed in the center of the room. If your table is pushed up against one wall, it is probably to accommodate the room's traffic pattern. This is not an ideal situation, because no one likes to eat a meal looking at a wall. Do you have to walk through your dining room to get to another room in your home, possibly your kitchen? Take out the leaves in your table or eliminate other pieces of furniture to see if you can fit your table in the center of the room. If not, consider a smaller table in the space.

Storage in a formal dining room is usually a china cabinet or sideboard. These pieces are integral to keeping your china and party ware easily accessible. These pieces should be placed away from the traffic pattern of the room.

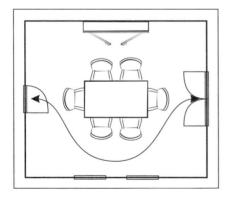

Think about what other activities you do in your dining room. Do you use it as a secondary office space or a project area? Maybe your children do their homework at the table. Does clutter collect in this room because there is no place to store materials for these activities? This is where you know best. Consider storage for each activity that takes place in this room so you can put items away quickly and your dining room will function well while being multi-purpose.

Lighting in your dining room has probably already been decided for you in the form of a chandelier or overhead light. It is ideal to have a dimmer on your overhead lighting. Being able to adjust the light intensity can add to the effect you want to create. You may also consider adding extra lighting to enhance the space. Do you have a large piece of artwork over your sideboard? You could use a light to highlight it during special dinners.

Room 3: The Bedroom

The bed is the focal point in any bedroom. Make it as inviting as possible. If you have an architectural element in your bedroom, it can share the stage with the bed and you will have two focal points.

Furniture placement is very important in creating a comfortable and relaxing space. You want to be able to move throughout the room without having to walk around your bed. To decide on the best placement of the bed, stand in the doorway of the room. Doors are usually placed in a corner where two walls meet. With your back to that corner, look across the room to the opposite corner. The best placement for your bed will be on one of the walls that share that corner. Choosing between these two walls will depend on where the windows and doors are located within the room. When you enter your bedroom, focus on a comfortable bed welcoming you into the room.

I recommend placing a piece of furniture on both sides of the bed. Identifying what kind of clutter collects next to the bed will help you determine what type furniture you need. After placing your bed and side furniture, move on to the

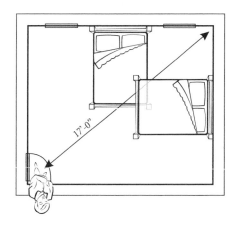

next largest piece of furniture in the room and continue until you have put everything in place.

Primary storage in a bedroom is for clothing. Make sure you have enough storage to have a place for everything. If not, you will need to acquire more storage or eliminate some clothing. You will also need storage for any other activities in the space. If you read while in bed, consider a bookcase next to your bed. If you need more clothing storage, consider a low dresser next to the bed. These items can do double duty by serving as a nightstand and storage.

The following guidelines will help determine if you have the minimum clearance around furniture in your bedroom.

- 19 inches on the side of the bed
- 24 inches at the foot of the bed
- 30 inches at the front of a dresser for pulling out drawers
- 42 inch diameter is needed for dressing the average adult
- 36 inches for dressing between the bed and other furniture

Lighting can set the mood for relaxation in your bedroom. It is great if you have an overhead light in this room for getting dressed. Additionally, consider having more intimate lighting in your bedroom. Place lamps on both sides of the bed and near a chair if you read, sew or work on your laptop in this space. If your room is large, consider placing a lamp in a dark corner to lighten up the area.

Room 4: The Home Office

If you have a designated room in your home for an office, the focal point will be the desk. It should be placed so that traffic flow to and from the desk is efficient. Your desk needs to be large enough to get the job done. If you write a lot or need to spread paperwork out, consider a large desk. I find that computer desks are not conducive to daily work activity. They are too shallow with not enough storage. When staging, consider where you want to sit in the space. Many people prefer not to have their back to the door while sitting at their desk.

Here are some suggested desk placements for a home office:

Move your desk and chair around the room until you are comfortable. You will be spending a lot of time in this position, so make it work for you.

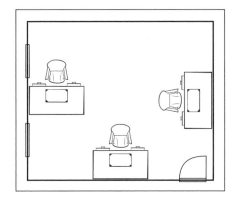

Home offices are magnets for paper clutter. After elim-inating the papers you do not need, which may be no easy task, determine how much storage is required. Most office spaces need storage for papers, books and supplies. If you do not already have one, you should get a file cabinet and bookcase. For maximum efficiency, materials you use often need to be within reach while sitting at the desk.

Make sure you have the minimum clearance to move comfortably in your home office. Here are some suggested guidelines:

- 36 inches for chair space behind a desk
- 30 inches of knee space under a desktop

- 36 inches in front of a file cabinet for pulling out drawers
- 30 inches of space to move around a desk

Task lighting is the key in any office. A ceiling light is great for tasks that require you to work around the room, but task lighting on your desk is a must for you to work comfortably.

Room 5: The Kitchen

Since most kitchens are built-in, I consider them to have no focal point. You can create a focal point in your kitchen with beautiful tile work or fantastic appliances, but I'd like to think that the focus of your kitchen would be the warm, comfortable atmosphere you create in the space.

A kitchen requires little or no furniture. If you have space for a table or a movable island, use a piece small enough so that you can walk completely around it. You can also place an armoire or baker's rack in your kitchen if you need it for storage and have adequate space.

Most kitchen storage will be in the form of wall and base cabinets. You need adequate cabinets for everything you use in your kitchen. If space is tight, you need to consider moving items that are not used for food preparation or clean up to another part of your home. If you still find that you don't have enough storage, you can purchase a kitchen island or adapt a dresser or bookcase to store extra items.

Do you have adequate counter space? Most kitchens do not. Here are some guidelines to help you determine if you have the minimum amount of counter space. These countertop requirements can overlap each other.

- 15 to 18 inches on the handle side of the refrigerator
- 24 to 36 inches on each side of the sink
- 12 to 24 inches on each side of the built-in range or oven
- 36 to 48 inches for general food prep

Lighting is important for a well-functioning kitchen. Overhead lighting is key and task lighting is also important at the counter, sink and stove top. If you do not have sufficient lighting, consider putting a small table lamp on the counter or purchase some under-cabinet lighting.

Now that we have examined the possibilities for staging the five most important rooms in your home, you will find yourself looking at space in a different way. By identifying the focal point and major pieces of furniture in each room, you can begin the process of staging. You should be able to find the clutter areas in each room and work to eliminate them. Review your storage and lighting plan by examining how you use the spaces in your home. This exercise will allow you to better function in and enjoy your home. Spend a little time experimenting in each space and you will create a comfortable, inviting environment in a home that fits your lifestyle and works well for you.

JANET SCHIESL
Basic Organization

Organize everything – simplify life

(571) 265-1303
janet@basicorganization.com
www.basicorganization.com

Janet Schiesl started Basic Organization in 2005 to provide professional organizing services to busy families, home-based business owners, downsizing seniors and the chronically disorganized in the Washington DC Metro area. She helps people gain the skills to get organized and live a more simplified life. Janet provides her clients with ideas, information, structure and solutions to help them gain control of their most important space—their homes. Janet gained 17 years of space planning experience while working at an interior design firm in the Washington DC area.

Janet Schiesl is a member of the National Association of Professional Organizers and the current President of the Washington DC Chapter (NAPO-WDC). She is the recipient of the Volunteer of the Year Award from NAPO-WDC (2008) and the Organizer of the Year Award from NAPO-WDC (2009). Janet also sits on the board of directors of the Association of Interior Design Professionals (AIDP) DC Metro Chapter and is a member of the National Study Group on Chronic Disorganization.

Organizing from the **Heart**

By Annette Watz, MARE, CDC

What is important to you and your loved ones? Do you want your mornings to run more smoothly with everyone in your family doing what needs to get done without any crisis or drama before you walk out the door? Do you want to spend more quality time with the members of your family and less time frantically looking for your keys, cell phone or the bill that needed to be paid yesterday? Do you want to be more relaxed and fully enjoy life? How can being more organized get your entire family more of what all of you want? In this chapter, we are going to take a look at how being organized is an act of love for not only yourself, but for your entire family. When you choose to put your attention on organizing your space and your time, you are giving yourself and the others in your life many gifts with immeasurable benefits.

The High Cost of Disorganization

Over the course of 18 months, my family and I moved three times to three different states. We left most of our things in our original home as we tried to sell it, and we moved into furnished living arrangements in other states. We eventually moved back where we started in our original home, which never sold, but with additional belongings. The possessions we accumulated over those 18 months just didn't have a place to be stored when we moved back. I was disorganized and discouraged. It was truly costing my family and me in many ways. I was often anxious because I couldn't find the things I needed that were still packed. It felt like we were living in a warehouse full of boxes instead of our home.

At first I felt stuck because I didn't know where to begin. My heart finally led me to our kitchen—the area where we spent most of our family time preparing and sharing meals. I began with one drawer and kept on going down the row of drawers, clearing out what I no longer needed and unpacking the boxes marked "Kitchen." I didn't let myself ponder whether or not to keep each utensil or item. I went with my first instinct and quickly moved forward. That first step catapulted me into further action because the success felt so good. My anxiety over all the boxes waiting to be unpacked was a gift in helping me to move forward.

Being disorganized can be very costly. It can rob you and your family members of valuable time when things cannot be found and of money when you buy things that you already have. Disorganization can also negatively impact your relationships and cost you your sense of well-being when you are stressed out, cranky or over-whelmed with all the disorganization. And perhaps the biggest cost is the loss of quality time with your family and time that could be spent focusing on a personal project or dream.

Take a moment to think about what your disorganization is costing you. Recognizing this can be a gift in itself. Recognizing that the cost is too high will make you more likely to move into action.

Perfection and Procrastination: Roadblocks to Being Organized

We all have our reasons for allowing our space and our time to become unruly. Often, we let our *procrastinator* and *perfectionist* sabotage our movement forward. On a regular basis, my perfectionist stands in my way of being organized. She tells me that if I can't do it perfectly, it's not worth doing. She ponders the best way to move forward with the project, and the options she comes up with are endless. She does her best to get me off track. If I listen to my perfectionist, my clutter multiplies because I am paralyzed with the thought of imperfection. If I choose to take action, remembering that organization does not equal perfection, I realize that it's okay to move forward because I can always go back and readjust as needed. I tell my perfectionist that being imperfectly organized is better than being perfectly disorganized, and she agrees. Remember, the goal of being organized is to have more time to do the things we love and to spend more time with those who love us even though we are not perfect.

Holding yourself to a standard of perfection can give fuel to your procrastinator. You know your procrastinator has shown up when you begin to hear in your head all the excuses that justify putting things off until a better time. Before you know it, the ten minutes it would have taken to put your things away has multiplied many times over and has now become a huge project. If your procrastinator is dominating you, take ten minutes to quickly organize something—even if it is your purse or one section of your desk. Remember one step forward leads to the next, and this movement will send a clear message to your procrastinator that the time for change is *now!*

Recognize that procrastination and perfection are not your friends. They offer you no value in organizing your home and your life. Notice when they show up, acknowledge that they are present and then send them away by taking immediate action toward your organizing goals.

Being Organized Is an Act of Love

Being organized is an act of love for yourself and for others. When you take the time to organize or maintain organization in your space and with your time, you are telling your loved ones and yourself that the family's well-being is a priority for you. The way you organize your space and your time can enable you to live in integrity with yourself and with your family. When you fall short, you let down yourself and others by eroding your self-trust and the confidence others have in you that you will follow through with what you say you will do.

I used to have a bad habit of putting myself last. I would say to myself, "If I have time to exercise, write or read for enjoyment this week I will", but something always seemed to pop up that consumed my days and left me with no time for myself. That meant I was not as happy and vibrant with my family. My husband observed my habit and supported me by creating a color-coded tool that showed every hour of every day. I started to fill in what I would be doing each hour. I committed to taking the time to take care of myself, and I scheduled my time to exercise and do my personal projects like writing and reading. I even included spending time with my daughter, working, sleeping and preparing meals. By seeing my activities on paper, I could then follow through more easily and say, "No, thank you" to requests for my time that just wouldn't fit in. I have discovered that when I follow my own schedule, I take care of myself. When I take care of myself, I am more likely to maintain organization in my home life.

Organizing Family-Style

I hope you realize that alone you can make a huge impact for yourself and your family if you take action. I hope you also realize that your impact can be even greater if you enroll others to help you on your organization mission. Enroll your family members into your cause by following these simple steps:

- **Hold a family meeting.** Get together with your family over a relaxing dinner, sharing your favorite meal.

- **Ask questions and listen.** Begin by telling your family what you love about them and how you want your home and your time to reflect this love. Ask them what areas they are struggling with, and then really listen. Next, ask them if being more organized could help them get more of what they want, then listen again. Too often as parents, we take on the job of problem solving only to find that our children don't like our solutions. Get their ideas and help them move forward without doing it for them. They are far more likely to take action on a solution they came up with themselves. For example, your teenager may tell you she wants more time to spend with her friends, but she has too much homework. Find out if it is really too much homework or if organizing her time or space could impact her getting the job done more effectively, leaving her more time to spend with friends. Ask her what solutions she can come up with that she could follow through on.

Your middle-schooler may say that you don't follow through with your promises of attending his track meets. Sincerely apologize to him, and then ask his help in coming up with a plan that will work for both of you. The answer may be as simple as writing the dates in your planner or entering them on your BlackBerry.® It may be that you need to be more realistic about how many meets you can attend and be honest with him about it. The more you can genuinely listen to and implement their ideas, the more buy-in you will have when it comes to having children and youth successfully following through with the plan.

- **Implement a plan, adjust as needed and celebrate often.** Once the family comes up with a plan, make sure everyone agrees to implement it. Keep in mind that you are the role model. You must follow through with your agreements and commitments if you expect your family members to follow through with their agreements and commitments.

Be clear about who is doing what. There will likely be bumps along the way, so be flexible to adjust the plan as needed. Remember to celebrate successes by commenting on each other's efforts and planning family events—movie nights, bike rides or whatever your family enjoys. After all, once you are organized, you will have extra time to do the things you love with the people you love.

- **Enjoy success and move on to the next project.** Make sure you have the time to enjoy the success of what you and your family created. Then you can begin the process over again on another area that needs your attention.

A while back, I asked myself this important question: "How can being more organized get my entire family more of what we all want?" I knew we needed a change in our morning ritual, because my five-year-old daughter, Faith, and I really struggled with harmoniously getting her ready for school. She wanted control. I wanted control. We were both losing, and we were miserable. We usually left our home upset and in a hurry to get to school on time. Since all of my ideas for trying to make it work had failed, I decided to ask Faith what she thought we could do to make this situation better. She knew right away that she wanted to make a job chart. In my mind, I envisioned all of the charts and stickers we used in the past that had only lasted a week because she lost interest, and I got tired of reminding her to use them. I had little hope of this being any different, but her genuine enthusiasm enrolled me to give it another try.

First, we brainstormed what jobs should be on the list, and then we used pictures to represent each morning's "things to do". She picked the graphics and I navigated the computer to drop them into the correct boxes. We found a place to hang it in the kitchen at her height, and she picked out the marker to use to make the check marks. That was two months ago. She uses the chart daily without reminders. She gets her jobs accomplished and is proud to check off her completions in the boxes. She will even give me updates about where she is while I make her breakfast. She loves that she solved her own problem and that I helped her to create an organizational tool that is right for her.

This experience has been so much different than our past job charts because it was her chart, not mine. It wasn't something I handed to her with a bunch of stickers saying, "We're going to use this every day to keep you on track." This time she conceived, developed and implemented it. Our mornings aren't perfect (remember organization is not about perfection), but they are much more peaceful and fun. Sometimes, we even have extra time to sit at the breakfast table and talk or read a book. We experience much more laughter together because there is an overriding sense of peace that she will get her work finished and that I will not bother her about it.

I now realize as I reflect on this experience that beyond the gift of more peaceful mornings, she is also receiving the gifts of building her character, her confidence and her own organizing skills for the future. She continues to grow more and more responsible with her morning jobs, and she wants to branch out and do more. Often, we will hear her say, "Mom, how about if I…" or "Dad, I can do that by myself." She is learning life-long skills that will benefit her forever. What gifts would you like to pass on to your children?

Until recently, I had not considered my ability to organize my time and my space as an act of love for myself or for my family. I now realize that my organization states loudly and clearly that my well-being and the well-being of my loved ones are important to me. I see that when I live organized on the outside, I am organized and centered on the inside. My heart is not weighed down with the clutter and mess but it is spaciously open to all of the possibilities and dreams I have for my life.

Each chapter in this book is a gift waiting to be opened by reading it and taking action on it. All of the authors offer you advice about how to live a more organized life in your space and with your time. Remember, a gift is only valuable once you open it and put it to good use. I dare you to pick a chapter, read it and take action! When the time comes, remember that being organized is a gift from your heart, a true gift of love for yourself and your family.

ANNETTE WATZ, MARE, CDC
Speaker, Coach, Fellow Dreamer

(612) 720-5770
annette@watzthebigidea.com
www.watzthebigidea.com

Annette's passion for dreaming and living from the heart impacts all of the aspects of her life, including her reasons for organizing her space and time. She believes organization is a gift of love for yourself and your family. Annette has lived in the suburbs of Minneapolis, Minnesota for most of her life and enjoys celebrating all four seasons. She also loves spending time with family and friends, especially entertaining them in her home.

She holds a BS in Elementary Education, an MA in Religious Education and is a Certified Dream Coach. Her most profound work includes partnering with her husband, Mark, on teen music projects which have resulted in multiple concerts and a professionally recorded CD of original music titled *Unheard Collection*. Using the Dream Coach® process, she helps adults and teenagers organize their lives so they can make their dreams come true.

Annette is available for speaking engagements for groups of teenagers and/or adults on a variety of topics, including how to successfully work with teenagers, how to get your teen or parent on your side and how to share your faith with your children.

Conquering **Kitchen** Chaos

By Tina Oscar

Do you find yourself serving prepared or fast foods to your family on more nights than you'd like to admit? Do you throw away unused grocery items simply to replace them on the next grocery visit? Do you waste time digging through cabinets or making an extra run to the store for one item and end up spending $50? Could you get excited about saving time, money, space, taste and waste? If you answered yes to any or all of these, your solution lies in getting your kitchen organized.

Most people are either intimidated by their kitchen or just don't know where to start. In my years of assisting clients with their kitchens, I've discovered that my clients just don't have the right tools in their kitchen nor do they have a system for feeding their family, whether large or small. Not investing in and not keeping the right items and tools on hand is like a painter showing up to paint a house without a ladder, brushes, rollers, trays, drop cloth or paint. What tools should you have in your well-equipped kitchen? Aside from the obvious plates, bowls, cups and flatware, let's take a few moments to visualize your cabinets and pantry.

Tools of the Trade

- **See-through, dry food storage containers.** Designed to keep moisture and insects out of your foods, these will also allow you to buy in bulk without waste, and to see what's inside and how much is left. For singles, keeping staples fresh until they are gone can truly be a challenge. Proper food storage is actually more important for a smaller family that consumes less food than for a larger family.

- **Microwaveable containers.** Nothing will save you more time than using a product that will allow you to prepare, freeze, microwave, serve and store your meals. It reduces the number of dishes you need to wash. You can also micro-cook foods in one-fourth the amount of time of a regular oven or stovetop, so you save valuable time and energy.

- **Square and rectangular freezer containers and labels.** Buying in bulk and dividing items into meal-size portions can be a huge time saver. When you purchase family-size quantities of chicken, pork and beef and divide them by the amount your family needs for a meal, you'll save money. Buy the largest bag of frozen vegetables and divide them into meal-size portions. Keep a container in your freezer door to keep that last scoop of vegetables that you didn't eat. Keep adding to the container throughout the month. At the end of the month, just add meat and you're ready for soup or stew. This concept will work whether you are cooking for one or ten on a nightly basis.

- **Bowls.** Have a variety of bowls from one-half cup to 32 cups. Select those with seals so you can make food in advance as "plan-overs" (food you plan to have leftover to use in another meal). At night, you can prepare the salad or dessert for the next night's dinner.

- **Appliances.** Most kitchens cabinets are bulging with too many useless small appliances people rarely use. Purge your priceless shelf space of all the things you really don't use or that don't serve multiple purposes.

- **Tools for baking.** Quality bake ware, mixing bowls, a rolling pin, pastry sheet, silicone mats, and a cake and pie carrier are all musts for bakers. If you're lacking space, look at silicone bakeware. It cleans up beautifully and collapses to fit into a very small space for storage. Have two sets of dry measuring cups, so you can leave some inside canisters of dry foods.

- **"Must-have" utensils.** It's worth investing in quality knives and cookware that have a lifetime guarantee. A good tabletop chopper is a great time saver and easy to clean and store. Silicone whisks, ladles and spatulas are all heat and stain resistant and clean up beautifully.

A Place for Everything and Everything in Its Place

Now that you have a well-equipped kitchen, how do you organize everything? I have to tell you, I'm not a big fan of pantries. I've found it's inconvenient and difficult to drag five pounds of sugar and five pounds of flour across the kitchen to the countertop as I prepare to make cookies. I've decided that my pantry works best for storing those things that I don't use that often. For example, you may only use the fondue pot, Grandma's turkey platter and chafing dishes for entertaining twice a year. Consider storing them on the top shelves of your pantry and free up a cabinet or two in your kitchen for frequently used foods.

I highly recommend eliminating all boxes and bags from your cabinets and using see-through, stackable, airtight storage containers. If you've ever lost all your foods to the infestation of weevils, you know how important this is. Weevils, along with a couple of other species of beetle, lay their eggs in the grains we eat, prior to harvest. They then hatch after the products have been on our shelves in our pantries for a while. By storing them in airtight containers, you will eliminate the possibility of the infestation spreading throughout your pantry, causing you to throw away every staple product and spice you have. Further, small amounts of rice, flour and other dry goods can leak out of bags and boxes, creating an attraction for more bugs. Don't forget your spices. They come in a container with a seal over the top. Once you open a spice, make sure to transfer it into an airtight storage container. Need to save space? With your see-through containers, you can stack your brown sugar on top of your powdered sugar and your tea bags on top of your hot chocolate envelopes. You will increase your available cabinet space by nearly 30 percent.

As you lay out your kitchen, think about where you would use everything. Your coffeemaker, which requires water, should be close to a water source. Above the coffeemaker should be items for all beverages: coffee, creamer, sugar, sugar substitute, tea, hot chocolate and powdered drink mixes. This way, everything you could possibly need is in this "beverage center." Pick the cabinet closest to your largest expanse of countertop to keep all your baking items. This "baking center" will house all the food items you use for baking, like flour, sugar, brown sugar, confectioner's sugar and more. If space permits, place your bowls and utensils related to baking in the same area. The "breakfast center," complete with cereals, pancake mix and oatmeal, a "snack center," with cookies, chips and other snacks and lastly a "pasta and bean center" housing your pastas, beans, croutons, lentils and rice will round out your centers concept.

Everything will have a permanent location in your kitchen. Imagine when it's time to cook, going to the specific "center" and finding what you need in an instant. Imagine, when someone in the family needs a food item, he or she knows where to find it. You'll never again discover that you have three containers of baking soda, all expired. You won't think you have an ingredient needed for a recipe, only to learn the box is empty. Grocery shopping will be so easy—simply open your cabinets and make your list. By looking at your see-through, stackable containers, you'll be able to see at a glance what you need to add to the shopping list.

UFOs—Unidentified Frozen Objects

The same organization concept you used in your cabinets will work for your refrigerator and freezer. Designating one shelf as your "dairy center" will give you a place for butter, sour cream, yogurt, eggs and mayonnaise. A second shelf can be your "plan-over center", to keep all leftovers that are going to be eaten within 48 hours. This will help you keep some semblance of organization. Rather than using my produce drawers for fruits and vegetables, I find filling the drawers with jars and bottles of condiments I don't use often is a better use of space. For the fruits and vegetables, I have invested in containers that I keep on my shelves that will keep them fresh for up to five weeks. This allows me to use my monthly cooking strategy that you'll learn about at the end of this chapter.

In your freezer, square or rectangular, stackable, airtight containers are a must. They will keep your foods from freezer burn—the drying out and loss of nutrients in foods that have been frozen improperly. For side by sides, I recommend using a separate shelf for vegetables, meats, desserts and pre-cooked meals or plan-overs. Make sure to label each container with the contents, along with the date, including the year.

But I'm Not Using that Right Now!

When you wash your silverware, where do you usually put it? That's right—back in the silverware drawer. When you wash your flour container, put it back in its "center" as well, even if you're out of flour. It will be waiting for you when you get home from the grocery store with the item to fill it. You can actually take this one step further, by placing items like your clean juice pitcher in the refrigerator. By keeping items where they will be used, you are more likely to use them than when you store them in a cabinet, out of sight.

Plan Your Meals to Save Time and Money

For singles, spending a day cooking family-size meals and dividing them into single servings will save you not only time and money, but increase the odds that you'll eat healthier, instead of just grazing through the kitchen at night.

The most common complaint I hear from people is that they don't have time to cook. Consequently, budget busters such as ordering pizza, fast food drive-throughs and prepared foods become the norm for dining. You can reverse this habit and get your budget and your health back into control by making a few simple changes. Would you be willing to invest one day a month to insure that you and your family eat nutritious and cost-effective meals for the entire month? I bet you would!

First, print out a calendar of the month divided into breakfast, lunch and dinner. If you have children who eat lunch at school, you might even want to pencil in what they're having for lunch. That eliminates a meltdown when they discover that you've planned the same thing for dinner that they just ate for lunch.

Thinking of your family's favorite meals, begin determining what you'll prepare for which nights. Be mindful of nights that are busy with extra-curricular activities by placing an easy-to-prepare meal on those nights. By doing this, you'll be able to have a variety of meals. Continue doing the same thing for breakfasts and lunch.

Using your calendar and recipes, begin to determine what ingredients you'll need to buy and the quantities. With the proper storage containers in the kitchen, you can buy the majority of your food—even produce—on one shopping trip.

Normally, the fewer trips you make to the grocery store each month, the less money you'll spend. Otherwise, those impulse purchases and end cap specials will wreak havoc on your budget. If you have remarkable self-restraint, you can actually save money by shopping the weekly ads. You'll find that one week, beef is on sale. The next week, chicken is on sale and the next week, pork will be on sale. If you buy a month's worth of beef the first week, a month's worth of chicken the next week and a month's worth of pork the third, you will buy when it's on sale and start a cycle where every month you replace your inventory with the item on sale. However, this system will only produce savings for the disciplined shopper who is not tempted by the extra bag of chips or other non-essential purchases.

Shopping Day

Get an early start on grocery shopping day, because the real work begins when you return home. Start by removing everything from the boxes and bags, placing them in their clear plastic food storage containers and putting them back into "their centers." Then, look at your menu and think about how you can get a "jump-start" on meal preparation throughout the coming weeks. Are you making chili, tacos and spaghetti throughout the month? If so, brown three pounds of ground beef, drain the grease and put it in the freezer in one-pound containers. When it's time to make tacos, you can take out the pre-browned ground beef and add the taco seasoning and water, pop it into the microwave and your meat is ready in minutes. *That's* fast food. If you will be making several dishes with a marinara type sauce you make from scratch, make up a large batch and freeze it in meal-size portions. When I come home from the grocery store, I always take a whole chicken, rub olive oil on it, sprinkle it with paprika, put it in my microwaveable roaster and cook it for six minutes per pound. Then I de-bone it and freeze several containers of cooked chicken that is ready for any chicken-based main dish or casserole. I use one container that day for a casserole for dinner and freeze the other three or four. For special events and holidays when I'll be doing an enormous amount of cooking, I pre-dice a few onions, several stalks of celery, bell pepper and any other ingredients that I know I will need diced. Then, when putting together recipes, it's a snap to grab one-fourth cup of diced onion to toss into a recipe.

Post your meal calendar on the refrigerator. In the mornings, before you get involved in your day, look at the menu. Take whatever you need out of the freezer. It will eliminate the "I didn't take anything out of the freezer dilemma." I call this entire process "cooking for a day and eating for a month" and it truly makes mealtimes a breeze.

Are You Ready to Conquer Your Kitchen Chaos?

Create a list of the tools you need. Empty out your cabinets, purging old foods and those small appliances that take up your valuable real estate. Using the centers concept, design a master plan for your cabinets, refrigerator and freezer. Challenge yourself to learn to cook for a day and feed your family for a month. A healthier diet, a more organized kitchen and money-saving practices will create a reduced-stress environment that will turn your house into a home.

TINA OSCAR
Custom Kitchen Planner

*Making a difference
one kitchen at a time*

(850) 346-0255
tina@smartkitchentips.com
www.smartkitchentips.com

Life as a military spouse means living on a budget and moving frequently. Sometimes, the kitchen you are "dealt" leaves a lot to be desired. With a spouse deployed for months at a time, being a geographical single parent meant that Tina was responsible for caring for the children and taking care of household responsibilities, while running an expanding Tupperware business. By using the products she sold and adding systems, she was able to conquer the kitchen chaos and create healthy meals fast.

"The amount of money and time saved is secondary to the peace of mind you have when you eliminate the stress involving the kitchen."

Thirty years later, Tina has built one of the top ten Tupperware teams in North America. Her sales organization has sold over $50 million worth of food storage and meal preparation products by sharing the mission of how to reduce the intimidation factor of the kitchen, thus conquering the chaos. As a result, customers can save time, money, space, taste and the environment. Residing in Gulf Breeze, Florida, her customer base stretches from coast to coast and includes overseas military customers.

Building Your **Perfect** Closet

By Toni Ahlgren

Quick. What is one of your first jobs of the day, every day, almost 365 days a year? If you guessed getting dressed, you are right! If you live with towering walls of garments squished together, leaning stacks of sweaters ready to topple, a tangle of laundry and shoes, it sounds like your closet needs an upgrade or replacement. The right closet will start your day off right, making your first task of getting dressed easy and efficient.

A closet with adequate space and proper design can have significant benefits:

- The ability to see everything you have makes choosing easier and faster.
- Putting together an outfit is a breeze when you know what you have and know where things are.
- Adequate space means clothes hang properly, allowing them to "breathe" after wearing.
- With enough space, garments also have enough room to shed wrinkles as they hang.
- Shoes stay nicer and are not scratched and nicked, thrown on top of each other on the floor.

- Cleaning is easier. With everything off the floor, a quick once-over with the vacuum cleaner is all you need to keep the dust down.

How to reach this nirvana, you ask? Start with a purge. Purging is a two-person job that includes you and a tough-minded-but-fair friend or coach who will guide you in the art of letting go. You can find more information about letting go and organizing your wardrobe in Gretchen Ditto's chapter on *Wardrobe and Closet Bliss* on page 105.

Assuming you have just purged and are left with the wardrobe you need and love, you now have the opportunity to create a space that will accommodate all your lovely clothes. Here is a short checklist of what you will need to do or decide to create the best space for you:

- Measurements of the available space
- Budget
- Choice of materials
- Call in a professional or do it yourself
- Approximate linear width of your different sorts of clothes: hung together, how much width do your shirts need? Your long dresses? How many pairs of shoes?

Your closet configuration choices vary from adding rods and shelving to an existing closet to getting a coated-wire basket system to installing a custom wood or melamine interior. Whatever your choice, your mantra should be "Go up!" Use every inch you can from the floor to the ceiling to maximize your space.

Improving the Standard Closet

Most of us have at least one reach-in closet, the typical one-rod, one-shelf model with sliding doors. One of the simplest things you can do to improve your space is add a shelf above the existing shelf. That is a prime area for wasted space, so double your shelving by adding another length. The depth of the top shelf should be somewhat narrower than the existing shelf so you can see and access what's up there. Adding shelf dividers to your bottom shelf will keep your stacks of T-shirts and sweaters from toppling over. These can be found at Amazon.com and The Container Store.

You can also add a second pole to create more hanging space to accommodate short garments such as shirts and folded-over pants. A second pole can be suspended from the upper pole or installed by a carpenter. If your ceilings are high, you can even add a third pole for out of season or rarely used garments. You can find the hanging variety in home or organizing stores. The Container Store sells a double-hang closet rod that you can install in seconds.

Another great closet invention is a pull-down closet pole, which sits up high. You simply pull the handle and the rod drops down to a convenient height. A gentle push and the rod retracts to the upper reaches of your closet.

Still another space maximizer is to use the less-accessible space on either side of the closet doors by building shelving from top to bottom on at least one side. You can tuck shoes and handbags into those spaces. Wire shelving systems are available in home stores, are fairly affordable and relatively easy to install. However, they are not always attractive and you are limited by the size and config-uration of components the companies offer. Bits and pieces tend to hang out of their wire baskets, making things look a bit messy.

The ultimate improvement to the standard closet is to rip out the existing fixtures and build a completely new, re-designed interior. Long and short hanging spaces, shelves, drawers and a hamper can all fit into that space.

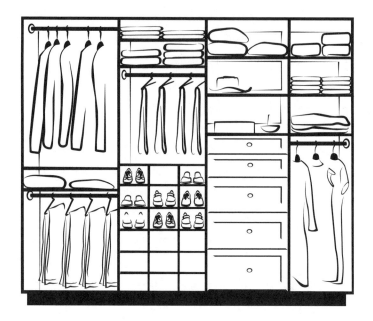

The Custom Solution

Now we come to custom. Your closet is yours. Your wardrobe and storage needs are unique. The advantage of custom is that you can make a space that works for you—not a space to match any one else's ideal. You can choose to build in wood, melamine or veneer. Melamine comes in a variety of colors and finishes and is ideal for closets. MDF (medium density fiberboard) is sturdy and can be painted or lacquered. Veneer is a thin layer of wood applied to plywood or industrial particleboard.

You have complete flexibility in designing a closet to match your needs, limited only by your budget and space. All these finishes work well, though the luxury of wood will cost significantly more. Regardless of the material you choose, you need a plan. Here are some things to consider and tips for planning the perfect closet.

- Measure the space required for the items you store in your closet.
- Measure the width of the clothes hanging in your present closet.
- Do you have lots of long skirts, ball gowns or coats? Think of the length they will require.
- Take into account how you hang your pants. Do you fold them over on a hanger or use a hanger with clips and hang them lengthwise?
- If you are tall, you may need extra-long spaces to hang your shirts.
- If are petite, you will not want to put shelves too high. If your vast wardrobe requires shelves out of your reach, simply design a space to tuck a footstool on the bottom of your closet.
- Do you have your shirts folded at the laundry? If so, you will want to accommodate them with shelving and save hanging spaces for other clothes.

Shelves and Drawers

Deciding whether shelves or drawers suit you will take some real thought on your part. You can get away with less furniture— bureaus, for example, in the bedroom—by designing shelves and drawers in the closet. If you have the room, think of storing your underwear, socks and workout clothes in drawers hidden in the closet. Sweaters can be folded on shelves or stored in deep drawers.

All shelves should be adjustable to accommodate everything from stacks of sweaters and T-shirts to flat items that require less height. Shelves can also be made with a short lip on the edge to pull out so everything is visible.

Drawers can fill up fast, so plan for plenty. I find that a few deep drawers for fluffy items like sweaters are handy, while shallow drawers allow for more visibility because you can see things in one layer. If you are low on racks or shelves, belts can be stored in drawers as can handbags.

Here is an important question: Do you want as much as possible behind closed doors or do you prefer the visibility of open shelving and hanging spaces? Door fronts can be solid material, either flat or decorative, have glass insets or be completely clear Plexiglas or glass. One or more tall doors can be mirrored for function and to expand the space visually.

Special Consideration for Shoes

Shoes are a whole closet subject on their own, but for now, you will need to know how many pairs of shoes and boots you own to determine how much shelf space they require. They should be off the floor on shelves approximately 12 inches deep. Shelving can be parallel to the floor or slightly slanted to give you a better view of the offerings. Shoe shelves can also have a lip or "shoe fence" to hold shoes in place and prevent them from sliding to the floor. They can also rest on deeper pullout shelves, two layers deep.

Your Very Own Island

If you are lucky enough to have the room, an island somewhere in the middle of the closet can be invaluable. Not only can it provide extra shelves or drawers below, but the top can be used as a packing area. Packing for your next business trip or weekend getaway will be quick and easy. Countertops can be the same material used in the closet or gussied up with marble, granite or a mirror finish.

If an island isn't possible, consider adding a counter somewhere in the closet. Close by the door, a counter can be a place to empty pockets, stash a purse, or charge a cell phone. If it's wide and deep enough, the counter can also be used as a packing station. You can have shelves below the counter and hang cupboards or shelves above it for more clothing so that space is not wasted. Again, you can be creative with the countertop material.

Seats, Fixtures and Lighting

1. Seats. Would you like to be able to be able to sit down in your closet? A built-in seat or space for a small chair can be handy for pulling on socks, tying shoes, etc.

2. Fixtures. Hanging rods, pulls and knobs, shoe fences, valet rods and hooks come in a wide assortment of finishes. Some of these are chrome and brushed chrome, satin brass and oil-rubbed bronze. Pick the one that matches your style, taste and pocketbook.

3. Lighting. Light sources should not be placed behind you, for you will cast a shadow on what you are looking at. Find a way to place lighting between you and your clothing. A small chandelier can add a fun decorative touch to your closet. Lighting can be placed inside cabinets, behind crown molding or be connected to a door hinge so that a light comes on when you open the cabinet door. In a small closet, even a small, battery-operated, stick-on fixture can help shed light on the subject.

There are strict safety codes regarding lighting in enclosed spaces, so be sure an electrician is involved in adding or changing fixtures. An electrician will also advise you on the necessity of a smoke detector.

Step on It

Don't forget the floor. Carpeting is the softest on bare feet and cleans up with a vacuum. Hardwood, laminate or stone floors are other options, and you can choose one to match or coordinate with adjoining bathroom, hall or bedroom areas.

If you use a hard surface, you can soften the look and the feel of the floor by placing a pretty rug in your closet. I've seen Oriental runners used to great effect in closets.

A Big Step Saver

While most homes traditionally have washers and dryers in the basement, off the kitchen or in the garage, there is a growing trend to put the laundry areas close to where you get dressed.

Evaluate whether or not your closet has enough room to accommodate a laundry area. The most compact solution is a stacked washer/dryer unit, but full-size units, placed side by side, may also be possible. A counter built above them allows for a folding and packing area. Don't forget that you'll need adequate plumbing and venting as well as that smoke detector.

Several of my clients, who had never combined "wash day" and "closet" in the same sentence, have made the switch. They now have their washer and dryer in their closet. They don't miss dragging clothes up and down stairs or across the whole house. They rave about this new, time-saving convenience.

Hooks

There's nothing like a handy hook on which to hang your robe or nightwear. Hooks can also be placed to hold handbags, totes, umbrellas and whatever else you use often or need to keep out and visible.

Do Get Fancy

Depending upon your budget, you can make your closet a design dream that coordinates with the style of the rest of your home. You can achieve this with the addition of raised panel drawer fronts, cupboard doors with glass insets, fluted column pilasters, beautiful pulls, knobs and crown molding.

Other bells and whistles to consider:

- **Pants presser.** Keeps those creases sharp.

- **Foldout ironing board.** It works great if you don't have a laundry room.

- **Mirror.** Make sure you have enough distance between you and the mirror so you get a full-length view of yourself. Place the mirror so that it does not face a window or light source. The light should come toward you.

- **Hampers.** Try separate ones for dark, light and dry cleaning.

- **Jewelry drawers.** Lined in a soft fabric, they keep your jewelry unscratched and organized.

- **Belt, tie and pants racks.** These slide out and help keep order and the closet visually uncluttered.

- **Valet hooks.** Pull out hooks on which to hang a few garments (tomorrow's outfit, for example).

- **Soft-close drawer slides.** A slight touch will silently and slowly propel an open drawer to close softly.

- **Hidden safe.** This is where the family jewels go.

- **Cedar lining.** This is a good bet for keeping moths away, but if you're sensitive to smells, you may not want cedar close to your bedroom.

A well-designed closet not only adds to the value of your property, but also expands your home's storage space. Most importantly, your custom closet will bring you the benefit of the peace of mind an efficient, attractive and well-organized space offers, every morning and evening. Get started creating your best space today.

TONI AHLGREN
Clearly Organized

(415) 444-5596
toniahlgren@comcast.net
www.clearlyorg.com

Of her organizing career, Toni will tell you that she just can't help herself. Like many other organizers, she was born with the organizing gene and has been programmed by it since she could put away her crayons in color order. Toni's idea of a good time in junior high school, according to a long-time friend, was cleaning up the friend's room on Saturday afternoons.

Acting as support staff in Napa Valley wineries, directing a non-profit and helping countless friends and family members get organized, she took the plunge in 1992 and started her business, Clearly Organized. She hasn't looked back.

A few years ago, Toni added custom storage solutions to her menu of services. Seeing her clients run out of floor area, they often needed to build up the walls to create more available space. Thus, creating double-hanging areas in closets, adding shelving where none existed before and using long garage walls to best advantage has become a valuable adjunct to Toni's other organizing tasks. She's delighted to use her creative design skills and her clients are thrilled by their newfound spaces. Toni is the author of two books.

Wardrobe and Closet **Bliss**

Your Key to a Happier, More Effective, More Organized You

By Gretchen Ditto

Fear, panic, nausea, desperation—these are all thoughts and feelings that many of us have at the very thought of tackling the process of organizing and cleaning out our closets. You know the closet I'm talking about—the one with the door that remains shut to keep everyone from seeing your deepest, darkest secrets. The closet that hides your over-purchasing and weight gain periods. Maybe your closet is not that bad. Still the thought of cleaning out a closet often means dealing with things you'd rather not face. It ranks up there with root canals and bunion removal.

Peace, happiness and confidence—these are the thoughts and feelings I want you to have when you go into your closet to get dressed each morning. I'm here to help you make that happen. Following a process to rid your closet of unwanted and unwearable items is necessary to get there. A well-organized closet can help make you feel like you could conquer the world. Your closet will be so well put together and organized that it takes you five minutes to get dressed. This chapter is the beginning of a new chapter in your life. Follow the process I've outlined and you'll find out how nice closet bliss can be.

So What?

Before we get into the nitty-gritty details of our closet makeover, let's identify why we're really doing this. After all, no one sees your closet but you (and maybe your significant other). Your closet is all about you and maybe it is in disarray because you're used to putting other people and priorities before yourself. Kids come first, work comes first and almost everything else comes first over working on your closet. Whatever the reason, many people tend not to take care of themselves or their closets. That is about to stop.

Why a Well-Organized Closet Can Make a Huge Difference

• **Saves time.** The average person spends 55 minutes a day looking for something they already own. I think it's safe to say half of that time is spent in the closet each morning trying to figure out what to wear. How much time could you save every day if your closet were organized and you could see and fit into all of the clothes hanging in front of you?

• **Saves money.** A well-organized closet will let you see everything you have and don't have. How many solid black sweaters or blouses do you really need? Did you even know you had so many? You love a skirt but never wear it because nothing matches it. A well-organized closet will help you know where to spend money and where not to spend it.

• **Reduces emotional baggage.** Checking your emotions at the closet door, ladies and gentlemen, is perhaps easier said than done. A cluttered, unkempt closet contains all of the things we don't like about ourselves and maybe it has some things we do like from long ago, like that prom or wedding dress or that old tuxedo. But more likely, our closet has clothes for our different sizes. Those jeans that looked great ten years ago that now can't get past your ankles, your favorite shirt in high school, that dress you have been meaning to dye for 12 years. Our closets can contain so many sizes, it's no wonder we stare and stare at all of those clothes but can still say we have nothing to wear. If it doesn't fit now, get it out of there. Clothes that do not fit only serve to remind us that they do not fit every time we look at them—and they take up good closet space.

If you begin every morning looking at an overwhelming closet, feelings of guilt, frustration and even depression are greeting you as you start out your day. I recommend you start your day out on a different note. Life can be challenging enough. Our closets need to become a positive force of emotional energy.

I am going to assume that you are motivated, excited and ready to create a clothing closet that supports you. I am also going to assume that you now would like some guidance on how to turn your closet into a sanctuary in the least amount of time. Here we go.

Prepare, Prepare, Prepare

Preparation is key to success and you need to take certain steps even before you enter your closet.

Set goals and objectives. What image do you want your clothes to reflect? Start by answering the questions below to help you stay focused as you make decisions about what stays and what goes.

- How do you want to feel when you get dressed?
- What do you want your clothes to say about you?
- What is the impression you want to leave on others?

Determine your "wear" frequency. Clothing you wear most often should be the easiest to see and reach. If you wear dress pants most often, yet they are crammed in a dark back corner of your closet, it causes frustration every day. Frustration causes stress, stress causes short tempers, short tempers reflect a poor image and hurt relationships. You get the idea. Reduce the frustration by determining the clothing style(s) that you need most often.

Number of Times You Wear this Category per Month	Category
	Athletic
	Sporty Casual
	Dressy Casual
	Career (job, volunteer)
	Daytime Dressy (church, luncheon)
	Dinner (evening)
	Cocktail
	Formal
	Special Events (weddings, reunions)

You can use this assessment in two ways:

1. Location within your closet. The items you wear most often should be the easiest to reach. That once-a-year cocktail dress? It should be in the hard–to-reach corner or another closet altogether. Do you wear career casual most days? Make sure those items are front and center, easy to reach and easy to see.

2. Spending. If you go to the gym every day, you can invest in comfortable athletic gear that makes you feel good. Never go to the gym? Don't bother with the $60 pair of yoga pants. Think of cost per wear. The more you wear an item, the lower the cost per wear. Thinking this way will help you buy quality over quantity.

Schedule uninterrupted time. Trying to find time to organize your closet is nearly impossible. You have to schedule time. Scheduling is a must. Interruptions can end up leaving piles and piles of clothing sitting in a bedroom, resulting in chaos and calamity when all you really need is a moment of calm. Take this advice: Do this only when you will not be interrupted by kids, significant others or phone calls.

Time schedule guide. Here are some general guidelines for how much time it will take you to organize each aspect of your wardrobe.

- Hanging items—two hours
- Drawers—two hours
- Accessories (jewelry, scarves, shoes)—one hour
- Full closet—four to five hours

Gather cleaning supplies. Cleaning out a closet means cleaning it out! Here is a cleaning supply checklist:

- Mirror cleaner
- Cloth wipes
- Vacuum
- Step stool
- Paper towels

Gather boxes or bags for trash and donations. You may prefer white or black plastic for the donations so that once the item is in you cannot see it any more. "Bye, bye old sweater that I wore on my third date with my fifth boyfriend!" Start with more bags or boxes than you think you will need so you do not have to find more in the middle of your sorting.

Create designated places for piles. Pile designation is important so that you can keep moving without getting frustrated over where to put items. Designate the following piles:

- Keep
- Donate
- Consignment
- Give to someone else
- Mend
- Out of season
- Don't know yet

You're Prepared—Now Do It

Let the fun begin! You must remain focused during this time in order to complete the job. Set a timer for as much time as you plan to spend.

1. Remove an armful of items, or begin by removing a category, like all pants, all suit jackets, etc.

2. Decide what to do with each piece by asking yourself:

- Do I love it?
- Is it in season?
- Have I worn it in the last year?
- Is it a great color for me?
- Does it fit me?
- Is it mine?

If you've answered yes to all of these questions, it goes in the "Keep" pile. If you've answered no to any question, then add it to the appropriate pile.

3. Clean the emptied area of your closet.

4. Return the "keeps" to your closet. WARNING: Do not put anything back in that you would not wear tomorrow. If it's out of season or the wrong size, it goes elsewhere. If you have a large closet that allows you to keep out-of-season items, then have a separate area for those. Do not intermix seasonal clothing.

Remember the chart you filled out about the categories of clothing you wear and the frequency? Refer to that as you decide where items should be positioned. If you only wear dresses once in a blue moon, then keep them in a back corner. If you want to wear your dresses more often, then hang them front and center.

As you return your "keeps," hang them by color, from light to dark. For example, all long sleeves are hung starting with all whites, then beige, then blues, and finally blacks. All pants are hung together, skirts together, etc. Hanging this way will be pleasing to the eye and will let you see what you have and what you're missing.

Keep all of your hangers the same in your closet. A mish-mash of hanger types is not pleasing to the eye. Slim hangers are excellent at saving space. If you have plenty of space, splurge with wood hangers. Get rid of wire hangers. Your clothing deserves better.

Consider folding items if space permits. I fold jeans, cotton tees, and sweaters.

5. Repeat steps one through four until you're finished or your timer goes off.

Your Piles

You likely know what to do with the donation and trash piles, but let's talk about the other, less obvious piles.

- **Don't know yet.** This pile is difficult, because you're likely not emotionally ready to give up these items. Put the items in a box or bag and store them somewhere else. If the item calls to you and you wear it within a year, then keep it. If you don't wear it within a year, then donate the bag.

- **Out of season.** In determining where to store this pile, choose an area that is temperature-controlled, like a guest closet. Avoid extreme heat, cold or dampness. I do not recommend using the area under your bed for storage. This area should be kept clear and clean, according to my feng shui enthusiast friends.

- **Mend.** Make an agreement with yourself to not put the clothes back in your closet until they are wearable.

Maintain It

We're not done yet. Just like anything that requires your attention, a key component is maintaining it. A closet maintenance plan will help keep your closet in a constant state of bliss. I encourage you to choose a maintenance schedule that works for you and mark it on your calendar. Here are some suggestions:

- **Monthly mini-maintenance.** A mini-monthly plan allows you to focus on one little area at a time. For example, this month I'm going to focus on my accessories, next month the sock drawer, the month after that is the seasonal switch. Mini-maintenance will take only about 30 to 60 minutes—what a breeze.

- **Move it around.** If you have all your pants hanging on the left side of the closet, move them to the right side. Movement will give new light to things and you may start wearing something you had overlooked. It's a strange phenomenon, but it works.

- **Keep a donation bag handy.** Keep a paper bag in your closet and fill it in between organizing events. A bag out in the open keeps it on the top of your mind. When you come across an item you realize is time to retire, just drop it in the bag and forget about it.

- **Clean as a whistle.** Make sure all of the clothes in your closet are clean. Look at your clothes before you put them back in the closet at the end of the day to make sure they are spotless. If they are not, get them cleaned before they go back where they belong.

Great Closet Organizing Tools

It is my belief that we are only as good as our tools. Here are a few of my favorites that can make your closet beautiful and help make organization a breeze.

- **Slim hangers.** These are super strong and save a lot of space.

- **Hanging jewelry organizer.** This handy tool hangs on a closet rod or on a wall hook. Clear pockets make it easy to see all of your pieces. Outfit coordination is a breeze when you can see your accessory choices.

- **Under bed storage boxes.** These are great for linens, blankets, and out-of-season clothing. Just remember to put these under a guest bed, not your bed.

- **Boxes or bins for shelves.** Turn your shelf into a drawer by adding a nice cubby box. These are essential for hard-to-reach shelves.

- **Over-the-door shoe organizer.** These are perfect for getting your shoes off the ground and in position so that you can see them. Do you have too many shoes? That's not a problem. Use the over-the-door shoe organizer for your frequently worn shoes, allowing quick and easy access. Display your other "pieces of art" elsewhere. Your shoes aren't pieces of art? Call me, we need to talk.

Other Helpful Hints

Reserve your closet for your clothes. Don't keep anything in your closet that you don't wear. A closet is not a dumping ground for pots, pans, curling irons, sheets or tax returns. Yes, I've seen it all. Your closet should be a sanctuary for your clothing, shoes and accessories.

Give special attention to your keepsakes. Store your keepsakes in an area that maintains an even temperature. Avoid basements, attics and garages. Wedding dresses and old photos need to be stored properly to avoid discoloring. Check with a local museum's curator for advice on how to store these precious items. Your local dry cleaner will often provide a service to store your wedding dress. A little research will go a long way.

Have his and her closets. Two different closets can create marital bliss but many of us don't have this luxury. A neatly organized closet is even more important if you have to share.

Create a photo book of your best outfits. Simply lay an outfit out, take a picture, print it and add it to a photo album of outfits. Keep this album in your closet so that each morning you just look at the book, pick an outfit and you're ready to go. No more changing your outfit 15 times before you're out the door!

Your Journey to a Happy Closet Has Just Begun

Our closets are a reflection of us. Let's begin by taking care of them and taking care of ourselves in return. Spend the time to follow this process and you will be glad you did.

Your next step in closet bliss is to understand how to transform your wardrobe from drab to "fab." This type of transformation requires a plan that includes knowing your best clothing colors and your best fit and style. You can accomplish this transformation by reading books and doing it yourself, or by hiring a professional image or style consultant.

I hope you continue on your closet journey until your closet is full of great outfits just waiting to make you look and feel fabulous. Good luck and go conquer that closet!

GRETCHEN DITTO
Ditto & Co

Transforming style

(612) 619-5820
gretchen@dittoandco.com
www.dittoandco.com

Gretchen Ditto is an image, etiquette, and style advisor who draws on 15 years of financial services corporate and sales experience to help each client project impressions of integrity, confidence and competency. Gretchen's unique background in consultative sales, marketing, training, coaching and project management combine to make her one of the most creative in the industry.

As an image consultant, Gretchen works with professionals who want to get ahead in a competitive environment and leave a strong, lasting impression. Her image services include custom color analysis, fit and style analysis, wardrobe and closet organization, and professional shopping. Each client is unique, so she customizes her style and wardrobe advice for each person's lifestyle, personality and body type.

As a skilled speaker, Gretchen provides her audience with inspiration, humor and actionable steps on the topics of personal image, closet organizing and etiquette.

Gretchen is a graduate of Stoltz Image Institute, the Protocol School of Washington and Arizona State University. She is a member of the National Association of Professional Organizers (NAPO), and the Association of Image Consultants International (AICI). Gretchen resides in Minnesota with her husband and her ferocious Jack Russell Terrier.

I **Love** My Office
Creating a Home Office that Works for You

By Angela F. Wallace, MIA, CPO®

Who needs a home office? Everyone. You might want a space for personal work, for kids to do homework, to pursue special interests or hobbies or to conduct a home-based business. You might be part of the 15 percent of the workforce that does some of their salaried work from home.

Can you imagine life without a command center in your home? We live in an information era and have information coming at us from all directions—mail, phone, fax, text, schools, work, books, Internet, family, friends, neighbors and organizations. Your life can be chaotic without a designated area to pay your bills, collect tax information, keep on top of social events and family activities, track medical information and generally contain the information that comes into your life.

> *"Simplicity is the key to brilliance."*
> —Bruce Lee, American actor and martial artist

Home offices come in many different sizes and shapes. Today, they might not even look like a traditional "office." I've seen home offices in the dining room, part of the family room, the spare bedroom, attic, basement, garage or even a corner of the kitchen. In fact, you can turn just about any space into a home office. The use of the space, not the space itself, says "home office."

Signs Your Office Is Not Working

Home offices are often identified by the paper that collects there. Where does paper collect in your home? If you have paper clutter throughout the house, your home office is not working. Here are other identifying factors that indicate that your home office is not working:

- There is so much stuff stored in your home office area that you can't get in it.
- You would rather work at the dining room table than in your home office.
- Being in your home office makes you feel tired.
- When you are in your home office, you can't find anything you need.
- Everyone else uses the space more than you do.

Less stressful households manage the information coming in. The truth is, today we all need some sort of home office just to run our lives. The four steps in creating a home office that works for you are:

1. Determining what you will do in the space and when you will do it

2. Identifying who will use the space

3. Deciding what you will need in the space

4. Discovering how you feel when you are in the space

Let's take a look at each one of these.

1. What Will You Do in the Space and When Will You Do It?

The first step in creating your home office is to identify the types of activities you will do in the space. Here are some types of activities often done in a home office: household and personal finances; children's activities like computer work and homework; family calendaring; investment management; writing; small business activities; crafts; travel planning; photo projects; Internet research and working from home. Your activities and tasks will determine the layout of the space as well as the equipment and tools you need. Make a list of all the activities and tasks you will do in your home office.

What days of the week and what times during the day will you most likely use your office? Here are a few ways that the time of use can impact working in your office:

- If you are working when it is dark, either due to a dark office or to darkness outside, then get the best lighting you can find. Full spectrum lights work best.

- If your office space gets direct sunlight, use window coverings to protect against the glare or heat. Your monitor is difficult to see in direct sunlight or with glare behind it. Also, some equipment and furniture can be damaged by sunlight.

- If you work in your office on days with noisy activities outside, protect yourself from distracting noise. Double-paned windows and background music can help reduce unwanted background noise.

- If your office is impacted by winter cold or summer heat, create good ventilation and airflow. Your office environment needs a comfortable working temperature for you to do your best work.

- If you have distractions from your household, locate the home office behind a door that closes. If you work from home, an office door also allows you to close the door and leave the office behind.

Bill lives in a 350-square-foot retirement complex apartment. The space consists of a living room with kitchen attached and a bedroom. Bill was a businessman before he retired and still depends on his computer. He needs to track his investments, use email to communicate with friends and family and do online research. In such a small space, setting up an office to accomplish these activities was challenging. The best location was the bedroom. Bill exchanged his double bed for a single bed and purchased a corner computer desk. The two file cabinets became bedside tables and the all-in-one printer fit on top of his dresser.

The bedroom had no ceiling light and only one small window. Bill invested in a pole light to put beside his computer desk. The light is perfect for all the computer deskwork plus the bigger projects he spreads out on the bed.

Pens, pencils, scissors and other supplies are duplicated on the computer desk and by the phone in the living room. Since there is no storage space, consumable supplies, like reams of paper, are purchased one at a time as needed. Bill lives his life doing what he loves to do and his space supports him.

2. Who Will Use the Space?

Determine how others will affect your use of the space. Does your home office space need to be shared with others—a spouse, children, pets, outside people? Who are they and what is their need for the space? What are the priority activities for the space? Sharing space can even be challenging with an animal.

Make a list of who else must share the space and list their types of activities and tasks. Prioritize the needs of the various users and allocate the space accordingly. For example, if the office also serves as a guest room for visitors a few times a year, the guest room space needs to be proportional to the other needs for the space. If you share your space with an animal, keep pet hair out of your equipment motors and protect the cords from being chewed. If sharing the space with children, keep the size of their space proportional to their needs for the space.

The most difficult space sharer can be a spouse, particularly if different working styles are involved. I know of one shared home office that the couple put a barrier down the middle so they each could be successful in their endeavors. If you need to share your home office space with others, make sure your needs for the space are met.

Mary, her husband and two preteen girls moved into a large new home. Her husband has a large home office downstairs. He works from this office four afternoons a week and manages their investment property and family finances. The room for Mary's office is upstairs on the main floor. This room serves as the children's computer and project room, the guest room with a pullout sofa, the gift-wrapping room and Mary's office. Mary oversees the children's projects, homework and computer work. She is a bank executive who works from home one day a week. Mary also takes care of her email and manages the family's social engagements and school activities in this space.

The work area is a desktop built along one wall. Mary's part of the office was too small to easily accomplish her activities. She consolidated the children's area into one-third of the desktop. The printer and scanner are shared with the children and placed between the two workspaces. Two small rolling file cabinets provide easy access to the files Mary needs and rolling cart drawers contain the children's art supplies.

Duplicate tools like stapler, scissors, glue, paper clips and so on are located in both workspaces. The children's activities are now confined to their section. Mary can easily supervise the children and everything she needs is at her fingertips.

3. What Will You Need in the Space?

The types of activities you do in the space will determine the supplies, tools, equipment, amount of space and storage needed in the office. Based on the activities of all who use the office, make a list of the things you will need. For example:

- Types of equipment: phone, computer, fax, desk, scanner
- Tools: scissors, stapler, paper cutter, pencil sharpeners
- Supplies: different types of paper, pens, tape, Post-its®
- Space: work space and storage space

If you work from home or spend a lot of time in your office, invest in a good chair and a large-screen monitor. Quality equipment is available at used office furniture stores for reasonable prices, and high quality office equipment can last for years.

Your activities will also determine the layout of the office. With a computer, think of the types of equipment you use with it (printer, scanner and so on) and create a space nearby for the supplemental equipment. If you do art projects in the space, what do you need available to do the projects? For financial work, what do you need to accomplish the tasks?

Once you determine what you need, use the following basic organizing principles to place the objects in the space.

- **Keep things where you use them.** If you have two workspaces, you might want a chair at each position. Smaller tools and supplies can be duplicated in each area in which they are used.

- **Group "like" things together.** For example, your various groups of "like" things may be books, computer-related items, types of files and art supplies.

- **Use the zone system.** The things you use most often should be closest to you and within arm's reach. The things you use infrequently can be stored farther away like the closet, top shelf, attic or garage.

At times, the space will determine the types of activities. Maybe you don't have the ideal situation right now, but you can make the most of the space you have. In a small space, focus on compact furniture and multi-functional equipment that fits the space.

Joann has two children, five and seven years old, and she helps her husband run his construction business from the home. They added on a large bonus room for the office and family activities. Forced into a corner of the bonus room was the office. This is the office for the business, which is the financial support of the family, as well as the household financial functions. Children's toys were everywhere—in their bedrooms, family room and bonus room. The children had taken over the bonus room and its large closet. Joann was spending one to two hours a day organizing the toys.

Since the children could not possibly play with all the games and toys, these were purged and only the age-appropriate ones were kept. Now, the toys and games are stored in their bedrooms. The children's use of the bonus room is restricted to computer use, art projects and some group games. The office portion is now about half the room and the closet houses office supplies and office storage. A second workstation in the room allows Joann and her husband to simultaneously use the space. Today, Joann comfortably completes her business support and home management activities. She even has room for new business projects.

4. How Do You Feel When You Are in the Space?

How the space looks and feels is the most important element in whether or not the office will work for you. This is the final step in the "I-love-my-home-office" feeling.

Make a list of the qualities you would like to feel when you are in your office. Some examples: calm, powerful, creative, happy, productive, successful, artistic, efficient, energized, focused, serene. No one thing can provide these feelings. It's a combination of the whole. Here are elements of the office that require attention to create the feelings you desire.

- **Visually pleasing.** Eliminate clutter in the space or at least keep it out of your line of sight. Use beautiful and inspiring items to uplift you.

- **Energizing.** Use colors that suit your needs, for example blue for calm, yellow for energetic, red for creative. Also, use lighting that complements your activities.

- **Music.** If music is an essential part of your environment, have a good sound system and music readily available. It can make the difference in the quality of your work.

- **Easy.** "Easy" is the name of the game. Easy to work. Easy to be creative. Everything is placed where it is convenient and easy to use. Easy to think, do and be. Easy to be in your office.

- **A place you want to be.** For you to love your home office, you must want to be there. If you do not want to be in the office, revisit the elements above to see what changes you can make. Remember, this is a process and won't happen overnight.

- **Customized to support your work style.** Personalize the space with items that are meaningful to you and support your work style.

Ron was running his high six-figure business from his bedroom using a laptop on his bed. The small file cabinet was full and all his important papers were in numerous tote bags and briefcases. He was always anxious about things falling between the cracks. A single father with two children away at college, he had a spare room that was no longer being used.

The spare room was turned into a real office with a desk, file cabinets and inspiring art on the wall. The room has a clean, modern look and feel. The walls are Ron's favorite color and a few of his favorite art objects made by his children are there to remind him of his reason for working. No more tote bags and extra briefcases. The important papers he uses daily are now filed. Ron wants to be in his office. He feels calm and powerful there and his business is flourishing.

Let Your Home Office Empower You to Succeed in Your Life

If your home is your castle, your home office is your foundation for life. Life is complex, complicated and changes over time. When your home office really supports you, you are better equipped to handle what comes your way. At every stage of your life, take the time to set up your home office to support you. The steps in this chapter will help with the process. A home office working for you will enhance your confidence and self-esteem.

"A journey of a thousand miles begins with a single step."
—Lao Tzu, ancient Chinese philosopher

Whether you are retired, an artist, a businessman or woman or you want to do projects with your children, a working home office can help you achieve your dreams. Start with just one step of the process. Follow with each successive step.

ANGELA F. WALLACE, MIA, CPO®
Wallace Associates

*Consulting, coaching and organizing
for business success*

(415) 897-5544
angela@wallaceassociates.net
www.workshop4success.com
www.wallaceassociates.net

Dedication to sharing her knowledge and expertise, passion for helping others and commitment to business success form the foundation for Angela's achievements.

In 1986, Angela established Wallace Associates in Mill Valley, California. Since then, she has developed a blend of consulting, coaching and organizing services resulting in a track record of client successes. Angela's special expertise in business development, organizing systems and workflow, combined with her people skills, make her a leader in the field of business organizing. Her clients call her a Facilitator of Miracles and Magic.

Through her Workshops for Success, Angela designs and presents workshops and is a sought-after facilitator. She has developed a series of products for entrepreneurs.

Angela achieved the prestigious designation of Certified Professional Organizer® with the inaugural exam in 2007. Only a handful of professional organizers have earned this designation. Angela serves as President-Elect of the National Association of Professional Organizers (NAPO) and is active in the San Francisco Bay Area Chapter of NAPO, the American Association of University Women and the Mill Valley Chamber of Commerce.

Conquering Your **Paper** Piles

By Melissa Stacey

Is mail stacking up on your kitchen counter? Do you find yourself making neat piles on your desk, but not really knowing what's in them? Have you ever lost an important document only to find it two days after you needed it?

I ask these questions because they are common issues people have with paper management. It is one of those areas that people struggle with every day, because they don't know what documents to keep, how to organize them or where to store them. We live in a world in which we are inundated with paper and information coming at us in many different forms. The key is how to effectively deal with all that paper and information in a way that works.

> *"Americans discard 4 million tons of office paper every year— enough to build a 12-foot high wall of paper from New York to California."*
> —American Forest and Paper Association

Benefits of Paper Management

Some paper is very useful and much needed; other paper is just taking up space. Paper management is essential, allowing you to find documents easily and efficiently when you need them, especially in the event of an emergency. You will save yourself a lot of time, energy and stress by setting up paper management systems that are geared toward your lifestyle. Just like anything else, give your documents a home so you know where to find them when you need them and where to put them back.

How Long Do I Keep Documents?

Do you ever wonder what documents to save? Many people are not sure what they are supposed to keep and what they can safely discard—so they just keep everything. This can be quite time consuming when it comes time to do your filing. Individual needs can vary, so check with your accountant for a list of documents that are important to keep and for what length of time. You will find some documents are necessary to store for tax, legal, or insurance purposes. These types of documents should be accessible, but don't need to be stored in the middle of your active files. Documents like these that are being held for historical purposes can easily be stored in plastic boxes somewhere else like a garage, basement or closet.

Sorting Through It All

Sorting through paperwork can feel a bit overwhelming, especially if you have large piles that have accumulated over time. Here are a few tips to help minimize those feelings of overwhelm:

Break down the project into "bite size" tasks. Focus on small tasks like sorting through a pile of mail, a stack of magazines or sorting larger piles of mixed documents into smaller, more manageable piles.

Set a timer to keep you focused on your organizing tasks for 15, 20 or 30 minutes, whatever feels manageable to you. During this time, focus only on sorting through paperwork, organizing a file drawer or dealing with your mail pile. While the timer is running, don't get distracted by email, the phone or people.

If you have multiple document piles, start with the most recent and work your way back.

Set up four boxes for sorting your documents:

1. To Do: documents that require action
2. To File: documents that require future reference
3. To Shred: documents you no longer need that contain personal information
4. To Recycle: documents you no longer need, but don't need to shred

Ask yourself tough questions when sorting:

1. Why do I need to keep this document?
2. Will I ever refer to this document again?
3. Can I find it somewhere else if I need it?
4. Am I required to hang on to this for tax or legal purposes?

Shred any documents with your information on it, including your address. Shredding large amounts of paperwork with a small home shredder can be very time consuming. If you have a large amount of paper, research shredding companies in your local area. This option can be surprisingly convenient and affordable.

During your sorting process, touch a document once and only once to make a decision. If at any point you think, "I will never read this" or "I am not sure what this is," then it is time to let it go.

Get rid of duplicate documents. If you have one of any document and you know where to find it, you won't need an extra copy.

Give yourself permission to let documents go.

Creating Systems

Having a system is the foundation for effective paper management. Your system will minimize the documents you keep and will help reduce the amount of paper clutter in your space. By giving your documents a home, you are giving yourself peace of mind because you will be able to find what you need quickly and easily. Here are some easy paper tips to get you started.

Mail. Every day, our mailboxes are full of coupons, advertising flyers, credit card offers, magazines, catalogs, bills and personal letters. Much of this paper gets piled on a desk, the kitchen table or countertops to be dealt with later. These areas then become drop zones for all the incoming paperwork. The documents intermingle, making it difficult to know where anything is. With the amount of paper we receive in the mail alone, it is not surprising that many people get overwhelmed.

To help process your mail, set up a central location for incoming mail:

1. Include a shredder, a bin for recycling and some sort of box or basket for action items.
2. Process your mail on a daily basis.
3. Sort through mail immediately when it comes into your house and get rid of the things you don't need.
4. Only keep things that require action—such as bills, notices and invitations—and process them at least once a week.

Magazines and catalogs. According to the Direct Mail Association, each year about 100 million households receive 16.6 billion catalogs. When sorting through magazines, catalogs or reading materials, let go of anything more than three months old. Only set aside current issues.

After reading, don't keep the entire magazine or catalog. Rip out the articles, recipes or pictures that interest you and create a "favorites" binder for those items. This binder can include products you many want to buy or research, articles you find interesting or ideas you may want to come back to later. You may also want to create a "gift" section, where you put pictures of great gift ideas for friends and family. It will make birthday or holiday shopping much easier!

By making a binder, you create a great resource book for yourself, you don't have to dig through all your magazines to find an article and you don't have to keep the entire magazine.

Check with local doctors' offices, assisted living homes or hospitals to donate the magazines you have already read, or share a subscription with a friend.

Junk mail. An average of 41 pounds of junk mail is sent to every adult citizen each year. Approximately 44 percent of this mail goes into a landfill unopened. To prevent unwanted paper from coming in, remove yourself from junk mail lists, magazine subscriptions, catalog subscriptions, email distribution lists and any other member lists you don't read or use. Here are some websites that will help you achieve this goal:

1. To opt out of receiving credit card offers, go to www.optoutprescreen.com

2. To stop junk mail from coming into your home, go to www.dmachoice.org, www.41pounds.org or www.greendimes.com

3. To reduce and manage your catalogs, go to www.catalogchoice.org

4. To remove yourself from email distribution lists, click the "unsubscribe" link at the bottom of the email.

Filing systems. Hanging file folders are a simple and easy way to store documents to which you will need to refer later. When creating a filing system, keep these tips in mind:

1. Sort documents into categories that make sense to you.

2. Create labels for your folders. Whatever you normally call the document should be the name on the label.

3. Alphabetize or categorize your files. Choose the option that seems most logical to you.

4. Position the tabs in the same location on all folders so your eyes can quickly and easily find what you need.

5. Do not create a "miscellaneous" file. If it isn't good enough to have a name, it isn't good enough to be in your file cabinet.

6. Purge documents from your files on an annual basis.

Don't bother filing papers you know you will not need later, especially if you can find it easily somewhere else. According to a study conducted by *The Leader-Post* newspaper (Regina, Saskatchewan) in 2004, 80 percent of what we file never gets looked at again.

Tickler system. One way to organize documents on which you need to take action is a tickler system. This filing system helps you track important documents by its future due date. To create a tickler system:

1. Buy a desktop file box and 43 hanging file folders.

2. Label the hanging folders 1 – 31. Then create an additional hanging folder for each month of the year.

3. If you have a bill that is due on the fifth of the month, then you would place it in the hanging file labeled 5.

4. If you have something that doesn't need action until a different month, like February, then you put the paper into the February hanging folder.

5. Each day, check the corresponding date and take care of those action items.

To do. If the tickler system isn't your style, just separate your action item documents from other documents by creating a "To Do" box. With this system, it is important that you work from this pile on a daily basis and have the highest priority items at the top.

To read. Create a reading area that is separate from the rest of your mail or action item documents. Put your "To Read" pile close to where you like to read and set a deadline for yourself to read these items. If you haven't read a magazine in three months, let it go. If you have built up a large pile, the "need to catch-up feeling" can take the fun out of the reading, so keep your reading pile low.

To file. Create a space for your filing. Once a week, every other week or once per month, file your documents into your filing system. Only file documents that you may need to reference later.

Emergency preparedness. It is important to be prepared in the event of an emergency. Gather your vital documents such as birth certificates, passports, driver's license, wills, deeds, financial account information, Social Security card and insurance information and make copies of those documents. Store the originals in a safety deposit box and keep the copies in an accessible, secure, portable fireproof box.

Kid papers and art. If you have children, only keep your child's school papers and artwork that are meaningful to you. A fun way to display the artwork is to frame them and hang them in your home. Each month, have your child pick out his or her favorite pieces for display. This way you are still showcasing your child's work without having the artwork take over your walls. For the other meaningful papers and artwork, store these items in a memory box. Remember: only keep those pieces that are meaningful and important to you.

School documents. Create a central location for your kids' school documents that is accessible to your children. Each child should have his or her own colored folder to place important school documents such as notices from teachers, event flyers, field trip forms, report cards, etc. Each night, go through the folder to sign documents and put them in your child's backpack to return to school.

E-solutions. Explore tools that will allow you to store certain documents electronically. Business cards, receipts, invoices and other important documents can be scanned and stored on your computer. There are a number of products in circulation that scan these documents for you. You can also avoid more paper coming into your home by signing up to receive bank statements and bills electronically. Setting up auto-pay for your bills to be paid automatically from your bank account is a great way to ensure your bills are paid on time.

Resist the temptation to print. A study conducted by Gartner Group and Hewlett Packard states that the average Web user prints 28 pages daily. That is potentially 196 pages per week or 868 pages per month piling up in your space.

Coupons and gift cards. Carrying store coupons, discount cards or gift certificates in your wallet or purse can be cumbersome. But these items are not much use if you keep them in a drawer. We often forget gift certificates or coupons until we are already at the location where we would want to use them.

To solve this problem, store them in a small document organizer or envelope in the glove compartment of your automobile. This will ensure you will always have them on hand when you need them and it is one less thing you will have to remember as you are heading out the door.

Business cards. Do you remember who this person is? Would you use his or her services? Do you want to form a working relationship with this person? If not, let that card go.

Maintenance

Until we live in a paperless society, paper management will be an ongoing challenge. In order to keep your paper organized and manageable, you have to maintain the systems you set up and be aware of your incoming paper sources.

Maintenance is about creating habits. But remember, we don't form habits overnight and sometimes we make mistakes. Be willing to forgive yourself when you make those mistakes and learn from them.

Also, evaluate your systems periodically to see if you can improve them. If you have trouble following a certain step, maybe you can change it slightly to better fit your lifestyle and schedule.

The most important part of paper management is to continue working on your organizing habits and be willing to change your systems if needed. Organizing systems are meant to help you save money, reduce your stress and give you the extra time to do the things you love.

MELISSA STACEY
Feeling Organized

We create systems that work for you

(408) 993-2237
melissa@feelingorganized.com
www.feelingorganized.com

Melissa started her company, Feeling Organized, because she wanted to find a way to combine her natural talents for organization and planning with her passion for helping people. Through Feeling Organized, she has been able to use these skills to help her clients find creative solutions to their business and personal organizing challenges, while also creating a successful small business and a fulfilling career.

Melissa specializes in organization for your home, office and small business. She works with each client to create a unique organizing system geared toward specific needs, lifestyle and/or work style. Some of Melissa's expertise includes filing systems, paper management, closet spaces, offices and workflow. She is also very active in the San Francisco Bay Area speaking circuit.

Being a member of the National Association of Professional Organizers allows Melissa to stay in touch with new trends in the organizing industry. She is a committed supporter of female entrepreneurship, serving as the Director of Finance for Women in Consulting (WIC) and President and founding member of Women's Networking Alliance (WNA).

Full and Busy **Family** Lives
Helping Your Child Learn to Organize

By Mary L. Noble, CDC

I am sure you would like your home life to be more organized, especially if your household has two people with busy careers and on top of that, a third career—raising your children. As a parent, you want to help your children grow into wonderful, exuberant, contributing adults. Too many young adults today do not know what to do once they are out on their own.

> *"The only things that evolve by themselves in an organization are disorder, friction and mal-performance."*
> —Peter F. Drucker, Austrian author, management consultant

As parents, we have two organizational goals: to organize a home life that works for the whole family and to empower our children to apply those skills in their own life. To do this you need to start with your children when they're young and help them understand the importance of organization. Give them structures that are easy for them to control and manage—structures they can apply to other areas of their lives as they grow up. If you can accomplish this, you will have served your children well. Allow me now to give you some tips to assist you.

The Power of Motivation

As you model and teach your children organizational skills, make the benefits to them very clear so they will be more interested in getting organized. Set up situations where this can happen. For example, if their toys are a disaster, ask them to find something specific you know will take time and frustration for them to find. Then, help them organize just that one thing and on another day ask your child to find the same thing. When they find it easily, praise them. Try this with a few different simple things and they will buy into the benefits of being organized.

Another important element here is to make these sessions fun for everyone, perhaps using stickers, new paint colors, self-selected storage bins and maybe a trip to the ice cream store afterward to celebrate the system you've created together. My now 30-year-old daughter, Carrie, recently told me, "I always knew why I was doing something and it was always done in a way that made the learning process fun and exciting." This is how you want your child to feel.

The Power of Time

Time is pretty ephemeral for a child. It can even be that way for us as adults. Some activities seem to last hours and you look up to see only 20 minutes have passed. At other times, it seems like 20 minutes and you find two hours have disappeared. This is even more extreme for a child. A good part of what seems like disorganization in a child is due to their different sense of time. As a parent, put special attention on teaching your child to tell time and where to look to see what time it is. Help them understand the concept of time and how long you would like them to spend on daily actions, like getting ready for school, clearing the table or feeding the dog. This will save you much frustration and help your children develop more awareness of time.

The Power of Color

Color can be one of the most beneficial organizing tools. Even a two- or three-year-old can learn to use it adventurously. Take a special shopping trip to help him or her pick out new organization equipment with color codes.

When I was a high school art teacher, I had no problems with cleanup time. Each table in the room had its own specific color of supplies and tools in a basket, so it was always easy to know who still needed to clean up. Each student also had a different color drying tray for paintings, so no one could say that they *accidentally* put their painting on top of someone else's. The payoff was that I could sit and talk with someone with a question while the cleanup went very quickly. This strategy is valuable for a child to learn to use.

The Power of Training

It would be wonderful for all of us if we could just tell a three-year-old or a 12-year-old to do something and it would get done perfectly and efficiently; but we all know it doesn't work that way. Recognize that when you expect your child to do something new, like put dishes in the dishwasher or tie his or her own shoes, it will be more work for you in the beginning. The first three or four times you will be working with your child to develop skills. This extra time pays off dramatically in the end, with more free time for you and a child who has learned a new life skill.

Specific Organizing Tips

I'd like to share with you specific organizing tips for four specific categories: spaces in your home, schedules, school work and living skills.

1. Organizing Spaces

- **Bedroom.** Even small children can make their own bed if it is simple. A coverlet that pulls up with a pillow sham on top will do the trick. Preteens usually hit a stage where their room gets to be a mess. It's the confusion of the hormones and their growth spurts. Just let them experience this with the caveat that the door stays shut so the rest of the family doesn't have to look at it during the week. Then, it has to be cleaned up on Saturday mornings. Most children of this age have no idea how to attack a bigger project, and this is your chance to teach them. Try this one Saturday morning. Get a cup of coffee or a glass of juice and head to your child's bedroom. Sit on the bed with your beverage and begin to give directions. Say things like, "First, pick up the books." When that is done advise, "Now pick up all the red things" or "Pick up all the stuffed animals." This is a good practice for breaking up big jobs into smaller ones and also experimenting with building different kinds of categories.

- **All over the house.** Ideally, encourage your children to pick up after themselves every day as they move throughout the house. If this doesn't work well, then on Saturday mornings give each of the children laundry baskets and send them throughout the house to gather anything that belongs to them. Then, have them put away all the items in their baskets.

- **Toys.** Cleanup of toys is best handled as a joint venture until about three years old. At this early stage, you are *teaching* them how to do it and they are helping. Make it a game, such as, *who can pick up the most books the quickest.* By the age of three, children can take over most of this themselves. The best option for storage of toys is open shelves in a bedroom or the playroom. Colored dishpans are the perfect size to store things: red for Legos, blue for puppets, green for matchbox trucks and so on. This way, the children can find what they want by themselves and also pick up more quickly because the dish tub is sitting right there where they play.

Keep in mind that no matter how good your system is, every child will sometimes complain and not want to pick things up. My solution for my children was this: "If you really don't want to pick them up, I will." However, when I picked things up, they went on my shelves in the top of my closet. When that happened, every night they cleaned up well, one toy or tub got moved back to their shelves.

2. Organizing Schedules

- **Timers.** Time is a difficult concept for many children to internalize. Maybe this is why four- and five-year-olds want watches. Somehow they see them as a magic connection to time. Go ahead and get them a watch, but get one with a timer or buzzer. If they get to play for 30 minutes, set their timer to go off at that time. Eventually, they will develop a *feel* for 30 minutes' time.

  Another good thing for this purpose is a kitchen timer. My daughter had one that looked like a frog. She took inordinately long showers, so we set the timer for 15 minutes. When it went off, she managed to kick into high gear and get out within five minutes. Eventually, she was able to beat the timer. Be aware that a timer with a loud tick will stress some children, so find one with a more gentle tick or no tick at all.

- **Planners.** By the time children start school they become familiar with time divided by categories, such as reading time, math time, and so on. This is the time to set up a big whiteboard schedule for them. Use colored markers and divide it into School Time, Play Time, Dinner Time, Homework Time and Sleep Time. Let each category be a different color. Make the box sizes big or little to correspond to time allotments. Let your children draw pictures in each box to represent what will happen. By the time they reach middle school, with some help from you, they should be able to schedule a day with soccer games, room cleanup, play time, dinner, homework and so on, with the actual estimated times it will take to accomplish these tasks.

3. Organizing School Work

- **Books and notebooks.** When I was young, one of the most fun and useful activities was to organize my books using color coordination. My English textbook cover, notebook and pocket folders were always blue, for Math they were red and for Science they were green. This made them much easier to keep track of. It also made it easy to grab from a locker shelf and get to class on time with the right book and materials. I encourage you to support your children to do the same and pick the colors that resonate with them.

- **Homework.** If your children bring work home to complete at night, be a good role model for them. First, help them set up their own work space as seriously as you would for a home business. Set a regular time for them to do their work. When they have finished, ask the question, "Is your homework done?" until they answer with the phrase, "Yes, it's sitting in my book bag by the front door." Keep asking the same question. Either they will answer, "Yes, it's sitting in my book bag by the front door," or they will take off running to do this.

4. Organizing Living Skills

- **Cooking.** Preparing meals and snacks with children can be a good way to review fractions! It can also be fun if you turn on music and dance or take turns reading the parts from *Romeo and Juliet* as you cook. Start teaching a child simple recipes and by middle school put them in charge of one meal a week. You can be the *helper* and by high school they won't even need helpers. Also, remind them to put things back in the same place every time. Nothing makes cooking more tedious than having to look for everything you need.

- **Laundry.** Every school-aged child is capable of sorting his or her clothing into light, medium and dark. My rule is that I only wash clothing sitting in those piles in the laundry room on the designated laundry day. Both of my children quickly learned to get their clothes in there, although sometimes they came skidding in at the last minute. By middle school, if they needed something extra washed like a soccer uniform or a favorite shirt, they knew how to use the washing machine and do it themselves. In high school, they took over their own laundry completely, and I gave them specific instructions so that they didn't turn their laundry load pink or grey.

• **Money.** Children can learn to budget money as soon as they are old enough to get an allowance or make their own money. Teach them to divide their money into certain categories: for example, college savings, short-term savings, lunch money or fun money, such as shopping with friends or going to a movie. Give your child some choices. In this way, they learn how to care for and be responsible for their money.

My youngest daughter was always missing the school bus even though we set a timer before I left for work. The solution? We took eight dollars of her *fun* money, put it in an envelope with the phone number for a taxi service and when she missed the bus that was her solution. She still missed the bus eight times that year but she was taking responsibility for it herself and eventually got it under control.

Everyone Reaps the Benefits

Follow the ideas in this chapter and your reward will be more quality family time and more self-assured children. You will raise children who can move on to college or into their own apartment with the skills to make their spaces comfortable, easily access tools or materials they need and prioritize their life, even their fun time. You will also, as a parent, feel a sense of accomplishment watching them mature in this way. Don't worry if they have momentary setbacks, for that will happen.

A friend once went to a dinner party given by her 24-year-old son who, when in college, had seemed to forget all she had taught him. But she came home raving about his clean apartment, the amazing sushi appetizers, the color-coordinated placemats and dishes and even the fact that the silverware was set appropriately on the table. Just keep the faith. The lessons you teach them will indeed benefit them greatly in making their way in life.

MARY L. NOBLE, CDC
Empower Your Dreamer

Living every moment in your purpose!

(937) 335-1766
mary@empoweryourdreamer.com
www.empoweryourdreamer.com

Mary has always been one of the lucky ones who loved her careers. In various ways she has been "coaching" all her life.

With a double major in art and English, she found it difficult to choose a career. After selling several paintings and prints, she decided her real calling was helping others and became an art teacher for eight years.

Her second career was a short break to raise two wonderful children. When she returned to teaching, fate steered her into teaching English. The most gratifying part of those 20 years was guiding individual students to realize and accomplish things they weren't even aware they could do. Along the way, she became a published author.

After 32 years of teaching, she retired in 2008, and became a Life Coach. She continues to write, create art, travel and help others. Her dream is to coach people who have the desire to help heal and unify our world. In helping their dreams materialize, she makes a large contribution herself.

Is Your **Garage** a Storage Nightmare?

Learn How to Clean It, Clear It or Cash in on It

By Bibi Goldstein

There are two general definitions for garage: 1) a building or area for parking or storing motor vehicles; and 2) a commercial establishment for repairing or servicing motor vehicles. Most garages are not used for either of these purposes. They are used for storage. What about your garage?

Think of the endless possibilities in which to utilize a garage: a space to park your car, a private exercise room, a getaway to work on hobbies and so much more. I have had more job requests for organizing garages than any other room in the house and I have learned that once you have a purpose in mind, diligent planning and preparation are critical. But where do you begin?

> *"Smile, breathe and go slowly."*
> —Thich Nhat Hanh, Vietnamese Zen Buddhist monk, activist, writer

The Purpose

It's good to have a vision for your garage's purpose beyond storing holiday decorations or the broken treadmill you have not used in years. Consider some possible reasons why you want to re-purpose your garage. Be specific. Here are some examples:

- I can save money on my car insurance if my car is in a secure location.

- It's convenient to exercise at home and I will do so more frequently with the useable equipment right there.

- It's great to have some 'me time' while doing hobbies and I don't have to be quite as concerned with the mess.

The Plan

Regardless of your vision, I recommend you create a clearly defined plan and stick to it. Here are some solid steps to help you plan.

1. Blueprint. Create a "before-and-after" blueprint using a standard letter-size sheet of paper. Fold the paper in half horizontally. Visualize the garage as if you have taken off the roof. On the top part of the sheet, draw and label what is currently in the garage to the best of your recollection. Be sure to draw any built-ins or unmovable objects. On the bottom part of the sheet, draw and label what you want in the garage—yes, even the car. Include any built-ins you are thinking of adding. This blueprint is only for you. Do not worry about details. Focus on the general placement of items.

2. Timeline. Using the back of your "before" blueprint, create a timeline to accomplish your vision. You can choose a helper with the necessary physical attributes, someone who is strong enough to help with lifting. This person should also be someone who will not try to influence your decisions. Determine who you can ask for help and set the dates.

Here are some tips to help you with your timeline:

- Choose a start date based on the helper's availability. If you intend to have a yard sale, consider starting at least two weeks prior to a desirable Saturday.
- Pick a date to complete the sorting.
- Schedule a charity pick-up date and/or a put-away date and/or a yard sale date.

I also encourage you to take "before, during and after" pictures along the way. This will motivate you to attack other areas in your life that might also need to be de-cluttered.

3. Preparation. Make a list of everything you might need. Most of us do not respond well to interruptions and having to go back and forth to the store is almost always the main speed bump. Buy extra. You can always return them later or use them for the next organizing task.

Here are some basic tools you will need:

- **Trash bags and receptacle.** Always purchase the large drawstring lawn and leaf bags. You may need to order a dumpster from your city or waste disposal company, depending on the amount you intend to get rid of.
- **Shelving.** If at all possible, line your garage walls with shelves. Most hardware stores carry industrial style shelves or baker's racks.
- **Storage bins.** For the items you will keep, use the same type of storage bin, regardless of size, to maintain consistency. If the bins will be placed on shelves, measure the interior dimensions of the shelf to ensure you purchase the right size bins.
- **Tape.** For sorting, use yellow caution tape or blue painter's tape because they are easily visible. Also keep clear packing tape handy for boxes, labels or other uses.

- **Boxes.** Use boxes for the donations. Clothing can go in the trash bags.

- **Labeling supplies.** Commercial label makers work well. You can also make your own labels with paper and a heavy marker (like a Sharpie®). Affix the paper label to the storage bin with clear packing tape.

On the emotional side of the picture, another aspect of preparation is to allow for the possibility that memories might surface during the sorting stage. Give yourself the freedom to work through any emotions you may face. Remain focused, but honest, about how you are feeling. If you hit a wall, take a break. Stepping aside for a short period can help you regain your focus.

The Sorting

The thought of going through the minutiae of each item in the garage can be overwhelming. Proper planning and a positive attitude can make the task go smoothly and keep your stress level down.

1. Empty the garage. The garage must be completely emptied so you can start with a clean slate. The empty garage allows you to use your imagination and creativity for the space's potential. Feeling inspired to change your "after" blueprint? Go for it!

2. Begin to sort. Identify a sorting area outside the garage, like the driveway or lawn, and divide it into four regions by using tape to create a large plus (+) sign. There is one region for each category below, except trash, which should be thrown away or recycled immediately. Make arrangements to have the no-longer-needed items removed the same day or the next day. This will free up space and eliminate the temptation to second-guess yourself. Commit to your first instinct. Once you throw it out it stays there. See Nancy Castelli's chapter, *Get Organized for the Planet*, on page 183 for important and easy recycling tips.

- **Keep.** Label each storage bin by its contents and the month/year stored.

- **Sell.** Keep these items out of the garage and put price tags on them immediately (see next section on "The Yard Sale" for instructions).

- **Donate.** Choose a charitable organization, such as a homeless shelter or mission to which to donate items. Take items there yourself to feel the positive impact of your decision to de-clutter. There are several charities that will come to you to pick up your donation as well.

- **Specific giveaway.** These are for family members or friends who have expressed their desire for these items. Place these items in a box with that person's name on it. Set a deadline and inform them that if they do not pick up the box by that date, it will be donated or thrown out, whichever *you* choose.

Start with large items first. By removing bulk, you will see an immediate impact. Clothing and paperwork should be last, in that order. What you sort in between should be based either on size or category.

> *"One man's trash is another man's treasure."*
> —Author Unknown

The Yard Sale

Having a yard sale can feel invasive and overwhelming, but extremely rewarding if done correctly and with the right attitude. Start your preparation early. Decide if you want to have it both Saturday and Sunday. You can also decide after Saturday is over whether or not you want to continue on Sunday.

Next, contact your city or county to determine if permits are required. Also find out if and where sign posting is permitted. Contact your local and regional newspapers to find out if they have a garage/yard sale advertising section. If they do, place ads in both.

Before you decide to move forward with the sale, I encourage you to write a contract and have someone witness it that will hold you to it. The contract should read:

I (your name) promise that all items that do not sell in the yard sale will be (donated to_____ , given to_____ , or thrown away) with the exception of (insert no more than 3 items), that if not sold, I have the option to place back in the garage.

Signed_____ Date_____ Witness_____

The following list of supplies is essential to the success of your yard sale:

- **Poster board for signs.** Most people choose white. Some have found that neon green and orange signs draw more attention. Place one at each corner of your block and one at each inlet from major streets surrounding your neighborhood.

- **Colored stickers for price marking.** You can purchase these with dollar amounts already on them or use a code system. For example, green = $2, yellow = $3, blue = $4 and use red to write in any dollar amount of $5 or more.

- **Boxes for multiple items with the same dollar amount.** This is used mostly for clothing, but can be used as well for toys, dishes, etc. Take the lids off the box and clearly label the price on all four sides.

- **Cash for change.** It's good to have at least $100 in increments of $5 bills and $1 bills to make change.

Pricing your items will take the most time and energy. Are you trying to turn a big profit? Your answer will determine how open you will be to negotiation with your buyers. Unrealistic expectations may leave too many items unsold.

Price all large items first. If you have a firm price, indicate that on your price tag. If you are willing to negotiate, indicate that you will consider the best offer (OBO means "or best offer"). On boxes, consider writing a multi-item discount. For example, $3 per pair of jeans or four pairs for $10.

Schedule your yard sale to start somewhere between 7:00 a.m. to 8:00 a.m. Be prepared for buyers to begin showing up about 30 minutes prior to the given start time. Ending times vary. Some are over within the first three hours after most everything sells and some can go on for multiple weekends. It is up to you.

The Putting Away

Follow your blueprint as much as possible, but do not hesitate to change things around as you go if needed. The important thing to remember is that everything should have a home.

Some guidelines to consider during this process:

- Frequently used items should be in easy-to-access places.
- Permanent storage items, like mementos, should be in less accessible places.
- Anything not in its own box should go in a bin with a label.

Do not be surprised if you find more trash or items to sell as you are putting things away.

The Completion

Now that you have completed your project, besides tired, how do you feel? How does the space look? Was your purpose fulfilled? Decluttering any part of your life can feel so empowering that you might want to continue to the next space that needs some work. Create a plan for all areas you want to organize. If you choose to do this without a professional, give yourself at least two weeks between projects.

Enjoy what you have done and recognize that devoting a small amount of time more frequently to keeping things in order will give you that same sense of accomplishment. By scheduling 15 to 30 minutes each week, you can keep things from piling up. Make sure to congratulate yourself on a job well done.

BIBI GOLDSTEIN
Buying Time, LLC

*Your personal errand and
organizing assistant*

(310) 376-1835
bibi@buyingtimellc.com
www.buyingtimellc.com

Bibi started Buying Time, LLC with a friend to provide the opportunity for others to have access to support and assistance with any task. She believes most of us simply need someone who is not emotionally attached to help us de-clutter various areas in our lives. In Bibi's experience, there has not been an organizing job, large or small, where emotions do not rise to the surface. Having the ability to focus on the feelings of her individual clients, gently assisting them to work through those feelings while always keeping the goal in mind, has served Bibi well.

With over 22 years in the transportation/logistics industry, Bibi has specific experience in space and time efficiencies through Six Sigma training for warehouses up to 30,000 square feet. This gives her the ability to visualize the final outcome even when her client cannot.

An active member of her business community in the Southern California area, Bibi is an ongoing committee member of the Manhattan Beach Women in Business, the Kiwanis Club of Manhattan Beach and serves on the advisory board for the Crown Jewel Club, a nonprofit organization helping at-risk young girls.

Relocation and **Downsizing**
Ideas to Make It Easy

By Katie Munoz

Is your home starting to feel like it is just too much to take care of? Maybe it's time for someone else to mow the lawn, clean out the gutters and cook the meals. Maybe you're thinking it would be a great idea to move into a retirement community, a gated community or a condo complex, but moving out of your home sounds like too much work.

If you are like most people who are considering making this choice, you've lived in your home for a few decades, your garage is full and your basement has more than enough. You love the idea of relocating and downsizing, but you dread the task of sorting it all out. Where do you even start? Relocating and downsizing can be a big, complicated project. The good news is that it really doesn't have to be.

I'm the owner of Moving Forward, a company that helps seniors and others relocate and downsize with ease. We have been helping people through this process since 2004. I'd be honored to share with you some tips that will make the whole thing easier for you and your family.

Where Do I Start? And What Do I Do Next?

I have found that it is easiest and most cost effective to move before getting rid of excess possessions. I know that sounds counter-intuitive, but honestly the easiest order of steps is to:

1. Sort out what you want to move with you.

2. Move it.

3. Sell and donate the items you don't want.

Why? First, it's easier to walk away from your possessions than to see them leave you. Second, there is less pressure to make the perfect decision when you know that you can retrieve a few items from your old home after the move. And third, if there is any possibility for an estate sale, you don't want to donate items that could be sold.

How to Approach the Sorting Process

Sorting out what to move with you can be quite emotional. You are embarking on a new chapter of your life, a new adventure. But you are also bidding farewell to the current chapter. It is common to feel both excitement about the future and the pain of letting go of the past. Feeling happy one minute and sad the next is actually very normal in this situation. Be tolerant and gentle with yourself. Allow yourself some time if you can. Sorting a few hours a week over a period of months is much less stressful than doing it all in a week.

Sorting can be challenging for another reason. People often approach sorting by saying to themselves, "I have too much stuff. What can I do without?" Then they feel overwhelmed and blocked by indecision. It is much easier to approach the task from the opposite end. Instead of asking, "What can I do without?" try asking yourself, "What do I use the most?"

You can try it out right now. Ask yourself, "What pieces of furniture have I used already today?" Did you think of the dresser, the nightstand or the bed? Maybe you used your television set or the recliner. It's easy to notice what you use as you go about your normal day.

Next, you can consider items one by one and ask this question, "Will I be using this in my new lifestyle?" For instance, if you are moving to an apartment, you know that someone else will be responsible for mowing the lawn. Although you use the mower now, you won't need it after you move.

Asking the two questions, "What do I use the most?" and "Will I be using this in my new lifestyle?" can help you zero in on the things to move.

Logistical Tips for Sorting

- **Labels.** Most move management companies, like Moving Forward, use colored labels to keep track of what to move with you. You can buy three-quarter-inch removable labels at any office supply store. Companies typically use green for items to move and red indicates items to be left behind for liquidation or donation. You can use other colors as the need arises. For instance you can mark items for family members with yellow and items to move to a storage unit with blue.

- **Clothes.** How would you tackle sorting a clothes closet? Do you empty the whole thing onto the bed? That's what my mother did. It seemed like a good idea at the time. But that big closet created a big pile on the bed. Then she was exhausted. She wanted to take a nap...on the bed, which was totally covered. Oops! Fortunately there was a guest room down the hall, but clearly there must be a better way.

You can avoid this by sorting from side to side. Put a red sticker on one end of the closet and a green sticker on the other end. Push all of the clothes to the center. Then consider each item individually and move it to the correct end of the closet. When you feel you have had enough for a day, you can just shut the closet door. You'll be free to use your empty bed for a nap!

- **Kitchen.** A similar strategy works in the kitchen. Just sort items from shelf to shelf and drawer to drawer. With this approach, you can take your time, and you don't need to finish a whole cupboard or closet in one day.

What Do You Do with All the Extra Stuff?

What to do with the extra stuff is the biggest question for most people. If you are downsizing out of a long-time home, it is likely that you will have a large quantity, maybe a huge quantity, of things you don't need any more. Initially, you might want to cart it off to the thrift shop to get it out of the way.

Donating is certainly a generous thing to do. However, the easiest *and* the most cost-effective way to empty a home of unnecessary possessions is to leave everything you don't want on the shelves and in the drawers where they already are. After you have moved out and your family has taken whatever you wanted them to have, turn the house over to an estate sale company. They will bring in tables, garment racks, locked jewelry cases, a cash register and set the home up like a store. They'll research antiques and collectibles so they can advertise them effectively and price them properly.

A well-established estate sale company can advertise so effectively that they can bring in as many as a thousand shoppers in a single weekend. Such a company will provide appropriate security for the sale. In one or two weekends, they can sell off everything from fine jewelry and furniture to paperback books and household linens.

Estate sales typically charge a percentage of the gross receipts of the sale. The percentages range from 35 to 50 percent depending on the quantity and quality of the items. Their fee should include all the advertising costs, the time to set up and run the sale and the time to research high-value items to set the prices accurately.

Some estate sale companies are also dealers and may offer to buy your goods outright and skip the sale. Personally, I see this as a conflict of interest. You are depending on the company as an expert to tell you what the items are actually worth. But if the company is also the buyer, they will want to pay you as little as possible in order to make a profit. When you pay a percentage of the gross, the goal of the estate sale company is the same as your goal, to sell items at the best prices the market will bear. Unless you are knowledgeable about the current market value of your items, you do not want to sell directly to a dealer.

Not every situation is appropriate for an estate sale. It requires public access to the home that a condo may not have. It requires sufficient nearby parking for customers and time to set up for the sale, to conduct the sale and to donate and dispose of the unsold items after the sale.

Don't Throw Away Money

As strange as this might sound—in an estate sale, the money is in the clutter. Yes, the money is in the *clutter*. Therefore don't clean up before the estate sale people get a chance to evaluate your items. Certainly, a successful estate sale will need some good collectibles or fine antiques, but to bring in the crowds you need lots of low-cost doodads as well.

Clutter sells. And while not everyone is in the market for a mahogany bedroom set, if you attract a crowd, you have a better chance of finding a person who wants to buy that fine furniture.

What sells in an estate sale? Kitchen gadgets, tools, towels, bedding, clothes, plants, costume jewelry, books—everything you would find in a garage sale and more. What about the things you just know are trash? Your granddad's old radio that hasn't worked since President Eisenhower was elected? Old photos of non-famous people? Toys from the 1950s? Old ration cards from World War II? Who would want any of that old stuff? A collector would want it. A person with nostalgia for a particular time period. A restaurant owner who wants to create a certain ambiance.

Some things sell for inexplicable reasons. One client had several shoeboxes of old, plastic dime-store horses. The auction company offered them in three lots, about 15 plastic horses each. Two lots didn't even sell. But one lot had a speckled pony and the bidding escalated. It finally sold for $850 because several different people wanted that speckled pony. Who knew? The collector did!

When you are downsizing, don't waste your time throwing things out or cleaning up. There are endless stories of the experts pulling collectibles out of trashcans and thinking wistfully about all the items that were already hauled away. Don't throw *anything* away before the experts get a chance to look at it.

Auctions

If an estate sale isn't appropriate for your situation, the next best choice for items that are more than 40 years old is to contact an auction house.

A reputable auction house will also recognize high-value items and take the time to research them and advertise them to attract interested buyers.

Like an estate sale, an auction company usually charges a percentage of the gross profit. In most cases, they require you to deliver the items to their warehouse. Be careful, because the cost to have the items moved could be larger than the return from the sale. You might find it more profitable to just donate excess possessions to charity and claim the tax donation.

Families Can Help or Hinder

How can you support a parent or family member who is relocating and downsizing? Let's say that it is your mom who is moving. First and foremost, be gentle! She is likely grieving the end of an era in her life. One of the worst mistakes family members make is to try to cheer mom up by saying, "Don't be sad. You're going to love the new place."

You would say that with the best intentions, but what she will hear is that you don't understand how she feels. She is likely to get angry or clam up. Commiserate instead, "You've lived here a long time. It is going to be quite a change." This gives your mom permission to feel the way she does and lets her know that you understand.

Second, be patient. Pushing your mom to make decisions faster than her comfort level will cause her to freeze up. Going at her pace will build trust. Going slower usually makes the overall process faster.

Third, no matter what, don't say, "Gosh, Mom, just let me throw out all of this junk!" This well-meaning comment is an absolute showstopper.

If she saved it, then it isn't junk to her. Now she won't trust you not to throw out her treasures behind her back. Instead, offer to "donate items to whoever can use them." Donate whatever you can and quietly dispose of the rest. It is human nature to look through rose-colored glasses. We don't notice the frayed edges and having them pointed out opens a whole new emotional cascade. Don't do it!

Charity

Some people equate giving things to charity as throwing them away. They know that they don't want it or need it anymore, but giving it to a thrift store feels disrespectful to the memories they have of that item. In those cases, finding a charity that helps individuals can be very motivating. We had a client who insisted on trying to *sell* her extremely worn furniture. She still remembered how much she had paid for it. When we found a charity that was outfitting an apartment for a recently homeless woman, our client was delighted to contribute. Knowing that her furniture would be appreciated made all the difference.

What Is a Move Manager?

Now you know some tips to tame the moving process, but if you still feel overwhelmed, consider hiring a move manager for part or all of the job. A move manager, like my company Moving Forward, will help you sort, pack and unpack. You can step out on moving day and come back when everything is unpacked, put away, the beds are made and the towels are laid out.

A move manager can handle the project from start to finish, or just do the parts you don't want to do. Most companies charge an hourly fee and will provide an estimate in advance. The cost varies from area to area. In Seattle, the going rate is approximately $55 per person per hour. A typical move costs about $3,000, but the cost varies widely.

To find a move manager in your area, check the Web page of the National Association of Senior Move Managers at www.nassm.com. Please be sure and call references to get a sense of the particular company's experience and skill level.

Now you know that there is a method to the madness of relocating and downsizing. You know where to start and how to sort. You know not to throw anything away before the experts have a chance to see if it is sellable. Best of all, you know that if it seems like too much work, you can get help.

The process of relocating and downsizing doesn't have to be a hurdle on the path to moving to a simpler life. Put the tips to use or just hire someone to make it happen. One way or the other, it is possible to relocate and downsize with ease.

KATIE MUNOZ
Moving Forward, Inc.

Helping seniors and others
relocate, downsize and declutter

(425) 702-8761
katie@movingforwardinc.com
www.movingforwardinc.com

Katie started Moving Forward in 2004 after the experience of moving her mother from a five-bedroom home of 40 years, to a two-bedroom retirement apartment. It was an enormous challenge. Friends and family repeatedly asked her, "What would your mother have done if you hadn't been there?"

Realizing that there was a huge unmet need in the community, Katie combined her years of project management experience with her passion for helping others, and Moving Forward is the result. As of 2009, Katie and her team of caring individuals have helped over 150 clients. They are known for their non-judgmental sensitivity, compassion and gentle humor.

Katie is a member of the National Association of Senior Move Managers, the National Association of Professional Organizers and the Senior Care Coalition, where she served on the board for three years. She is a regular speaker with ElderMove Alliance and has been a panelist at the annual Housing Resource Fair.

Moving Forward serves the Seattle metropolitan area and would love to serve you!

Celebrations in Your Home
Planning with Ease and Enjoyment

By Scott Roewer, CPO®

I believe a delightful party experience is possible when people feel good, are relaxed and are socially engaged with others. This trio of success is easy to achieve for an organized host. If you'd like to have organized celebrations in your home and want to have fun at your own party, keep reading!

Find a Reason

The first step to having a successful event is to have a reason for your celebration. Why do you want to have a party? Perhaps it is to acknowledge a holiday or your child's high school graduation. Perhaps it's a housewarming party or simply because you're anticipating beautiful weather. Whatever the reason or occasion, start from that place.

Next, determine the type of party you will host. Will it be a lunch, a brunch, a big bash, a cocktail party? Will it be formal or casual? Decide on the type of party and the general vibe or mood of your party. Make sure the vibe matches the reason you're hosting a party.

If you have hosted a party in the past and did not have the opportunity to enjoy your event, perhaps it was a lack of advanced planning. You're encouraged to enjoy your event and this can be achieved with careful preparation. Eliminate stress by reminding yourself you would like to enjoy the celebration, too. Focus on this when organizing your special event. The key is to take care of everything in advance so you can be a calm, cool and relaxed host. If planning is not your forte, I recommend that you keep it simple so you can be both a wonderful host and a social participant. A simple gathering is better than having an elaborate celebration where your guests are not able to spend time with you because you're too busy working.

Once you have your reason and the type and vibe for your party in mind, it's time to start thinking about your budget.

Planning Your Budget While Maintaining Style and Taste

A carefully planned budget will be your go-to guide for planning. The budget affects everything from location, décor, theme, food, beverage options and the number of people you'll invite. Having a fantastic party that creates wonderful memories does not mean you must spend a fortune. Yet, no matter the size of your budget, enhance your event with style and taste.

When creating your budget, consider the following elements when establishing ideas and formalizing your goals. Strive to consume all the senses of your guests. I want them to relish the sights of the décor and the lighting. After all, seeing is feeling. Lighting can instantly change the vibe of your party. Guests will enjoy hearing something besides constant chatter. Pre-select your music mix to support your celebration. Your entertainment will help your guests unwind, stir joy or transfer your guests to a different mental state. The sense of smell is also powerful. Guests can indulge in the aroma and savor the taste of the food and beverage options provided. Unscented candles are recommended, as to not distract from the fragrance of the food. Finally, every guest wants to feel or experience the party. By organizing your event in advance, you'll have time to socialize with everyone. Your guests will be delighted you've opened your home to share time with them. Capitalize on their senses and you will surpass all of your guests' expectations, even on a modest budget.

Begin your budget planning by making a list of the various expenses you anticipate for your party. This should include invitations, food, beverage, decorations, entertainment, hired help, rental fees, etc. Be realistic with what you can afford. If you find the need to slim down your expenses, determine what is most important to you and scale back from there. Just remember that great décor and entertainment + not enough food and beverage = a poorly planned celebration.

Finding Cheap Help

If you're hosting a large event, it is often necessary to hire outside assistance. Hire local, cash-strapped college students to pour drinks, pick up after your guests, check coats or help with yard work to prepare the back yard for a festive summer barbecue.

I've hired a client's favorite waiter from a restaurant to serve food and pass hors d'oeuvres. I've even contacted a bartending school to find someone in training to bartend in-home events. If you are having more than a few guests, invest in some help to ensure you do not spend the whole evening in the kitchen.

Planning the Beverages

Planning your beverage menu ties directly into your budget and the flow of your celebration. Do you imagine you'll have a full bar or does your budget encourage the concept of a signature drink? Will you have the help to manage a full bar or will there be space for guests to pour their own drinks? Perhaps a few strategically placed pitchers with a colorful cocktail will facilitate a more fluid flow at your event. Either way, planning ahead will help you stay on budget.

You'll save considerable funds if you have a signature cocktail or two for your guests rather than providing a plethora of beverage options. You'll also save time, because you can make these cocktails in advance.

Make sure your beverage options match your theme and that they are beverages everyone will want to drink. For example, serving Pink Cosmos at your next Super Bowl party likely would not work.

If you have a tight budget, but are planning an open bar, pour the liquor into funky pitchers or bottles and create your own custom labels. By doing so, you can disguise that you bought the industrial-size bottles from the warehouse store or that you bought the budget brand of vodka.

Make a list of all the items you'll need. Be sure to include liquor, mixers, garnishes, corkscrews, ice buckets, ice, mixing straws, beverage napkins, etc. Don't forget non-alcoholic beverages for your guests. Also, be sure to check that you'll have enough barware. Will you want to re-use glasses for your guests or will you want to serve additional drinks in a fresh glass? If you will serve multiple red wines, do you have enough glasses? Perhaps plastic cups are ideal for your event. Either way, planning ahead will prevent any last minute frustration for you, enable you to stay on budget and allow you to enjoy the party with your guests.

Determining the amount of liquor required for a party can be tricky. If you're working with a caterer or a hotel, they can help you estimate the total cost. If you're planning the celebration, start with the number of guests you'll entertain. Remember, people will drink more in the evening vs. a mid-afternoon lunch. If the party is outside on a hot day, or if you serve spicy or salty foods, your guests will drink more. Consider the length of your party. Two hours of liquor is considerably cheaper than providing beverages for four hours. On average, a bottle of wine will serve four glasses. Cocktails poured "properly" will have 1.5 ounces per drink.

Use the average of two drinks per hour, per person for the first two hours, followed by one drink per hour after that. If your friends are like mine and they enjoy their liquid libations, you may need to double those estimates if hosting an evening event. Also consider the mixers, ice and the size of your glasses. Utilizing a bartender who mixes the beverages will ensure your liquor lasts longer. If you're computer savvy, use Google to look up "how much liquor to buy for a party." You'll find links to several handy drink estimation calculators.

One final thought: If you're serving alcohol, please do so responsibly. Be cautious of guests who are overindulging. Have the phone number for a local taxi service or offer a guest room to a couple who may have enjoyed the party more than anticipated.

Selecting the Date and Time

Having your party on the right date is very important. The date selection will correlate with your planning. I always recommend clients avoid major holidays and religious celebrations because people plan their vacations around these dates. Requesting they attend your celebration on those special days requires advance planning. If you'll be having a party on a major holiday or during the busy holiday party season, send out a "Save the Date" card or email announcing your party one or two months in advance.

The start time of your party directly affects the kind of party you're hosting. For example, if you're celebrating a young child's birthday party, a mid-afternoon start time might be ideal. If you are celebrating Grandma's 80th birthday, starting at 8:00 p.m. on a Saturday night might not be ideal if she's usually asleep on the sofa by 9:00 p.m. One important rule when planning the length of your event is simple—leave your guests wanting more. End at the right time and your sanity will thank you later.

Location, Location, Location

Selecting the right venue is key in making your event a success. I've held successful parties for clients in restaurants, hotels, private dance clubs, churches, tents, public parks and their neighbor's back yard. Wherever you host your party, careful planning will allow you to enjoy the event.

Most parties will be in your home, which is ideal for the most intimate occasions. When selecting an off-site venue, consider the number of guests you will invite. Is transportation easily available for everyone to get there? Is there sufficient parking or will you need to hire a valet? Is there enough space for a nice flow to your event? Are there amenities offered that you can use? Are you able to bring your own support staff? Don't forget this all affects your budget.

Party at Your Place

If your party is in your home, you'll need to prepare your home. If your budget is flexible, move out some of your larger pieces of furniture into the garage or a guest room and rent some party-specific tables and furniture. For example, a few strategically placed high-top cocktail tables with linens to support your theme will allow your guests to easily move through your space and have a place to mingle. Perhaps a long buffet table with food service on two sides is ideal for your gathering.

If renting is not in your budget, work with what you have or borrow from a friend. If you need more space, you can still move out pieces of furniture to allow for better traffic flow.

Party Proofing Your Home

Part of your planning process needs to include the preparation of your home, both on the inside and out. A few days before the arrival of your guests, grab a laundry basket and do a general sweep for random clutter. Eliminate any papers, magazines, pet toys, items left out by your spouse, etc. If you have time, put these items in their appropriate places. If you're behind in your planning, you may need to schedule a post-celebration time to organize this basket of clutter.

If you'll be hosting an outdoor event, make sure your patio furniture is in tiptop shape. Plastic furniture may need to be cleaned and wood furniture may need to be checked for loose hardware. You wouldn't want any party mishaps because of a lack of planning on your part. Inviting guests to bring their own seating to your outdoor party will allow you to save money by not renting additional seating.

We've all found guests snooping around our homes no matter how hard you try to block off a space. As a general rule, remember that no room in your home will be off limits. Make sure each bathroom is stocked with soap and tissue. I recommend a stack of nice paper napkins for guests to dry off their hands instead of towels. If you have personal items or medication in the bathroom, remove those items.

If guests' coats will be stored in a bedroom, remove or hide all personal items. Guests may be curious to sneak a peek in your closet while they gather their coats to leave.

Remember that kitchens are often the busiest place during a party. Clear the counters of unnecessary items and remove all paper. The one time you leave something on the counter will be the one time a guest spills a cocktail.

If your celebration will include children, have a kids' area for food that contains kid-friendly snacks. A special play area may need to be set up for the kids. If your children do not want to share all their toys, be sure to remove any toys that are not for the entire group. This will prevent arguments. If your budget allows, consider having childcare assistance so the adults can enjoy themselves while the kids remain under adult supervision.

Can your guests easily find the house numbers? Consider a marker outside that shouts, "Hey, the party is here!" This could be as simple as balloons outside your home for a children's party or spooky lighting for a festive Halloween celebration.

When preparing the outside of your home, it's important to clear the driveway of garbage cans, toys and any random items that may have landed there. Are there dead potted plants, leftover holiday décor or has trash blown into the yard? If so, now is your opportunity to spruce up the yard. Don't forget to mow the yard and bag the grass. Grass cuttings can be tracked into your house and may stir up your guests' allergies.

Will your pets be comfortable in a house full of people? Maybe you can schedule a doggy play date or make a reservation at a pet hotel for your cats. If that's not in the budget, remember to have a bone or new toy to occupy your pet during the event.

Parking

Hosting parties means you'll be bringing guests into your neighborhood and parking may be difficult. Be considerate and notify your neighbors of the party. If you're inviting your neighbors, ask if you can move your cars into their driveway. If your budget allows, consider hiring a valet. Make sure the valet company has proper insurance. Have a meeting with the valet company prior to the party so they understand the logistics, which may alleviate any last-minute stress for you and your guests. Finally, call your insurance provider to verify if you need any additional coverage for the party. One valet per ten cars is a good rule of thumb when determining your needs.

Your Jobs as Host

As the celebration host, you're the producer, creator, head honcho, boss, queen bee, diva, coordinator and more. Whatever title you select for yourself, keep in mind that you set the vision, energy and tone for the event you desire.

Previously in this chapter, I provided you with numerous guidelines for your event. Take this opportunity to create a timeline now. Your lead time is influenced by the type of party. Casual events require less preparation time. Hosting parties on major holidays or special dates requires months of planning. Here's a general timeline for a dinner party in your home.

Dinner Party Sample Timeline

Four Weeks Out

- Select your date for your dinner party

Three Weeks Out

- Plan your food and drink menu for the event
- Send out the invitations (electronic, phone or mailed)

Two Weeks Out

- If renting equipment/furniture, make the reservations
- Brainstorm ideas for décor
- Select your attire for your event
- Make your shopping list based on your menu

One Week Out

- Review the guest list
- Phone anyone who has not responded to the RSVP
- Purchase all food and beverage items on your shopping list
- Prep any food that you can cook and freeze
- Purchase any items you need for your décor

Two Days Out

- Begin decorating your space
- Clean and de-clutter the space

- If you hate cleaning, hire a cleaning crew
- Gather all serving pieces
- Place a sticky note in each dish designating what will be served in the dish
- Pair flatware with each dish

One Day Before

- Fresh flowers should be delivered or create your arrangements
- Set the table and involve your family in the process if you need help
- Finish the decorations
- Meet with bartender, valet or any hired staff and share your expectations for your evening
- Finalize your attire by gathering all clothing, jewelry, shoes, etc.
- Because you've planned so well, maybe you'll have time to have your nails done, get a massage or meet a friend for coffee.

Entertaining does not require a great deal of time, an army of help or the skills of Martha Stewart. The aspiration to share your home, your passionate attitude and desire to be hospitable with others will provide an ideal starting place for planning your celebration. Follow the ideas and steps we have discussed and next time, both you *and* your guests will have a fun and memorable time.

SCOTT ROEWER, CPO®
Solutions by Scott, LLC

(202) 249-8330
scott@solutionsbyscott.com
www.solutionsbyscott.com
www.declutteryou.com

Based in Washington, DC, Certified Professional Organizer® Scott Roewer believes that everyone can live a more organized life. Scott believes that organizing a space is easy, but organizing a person requires a professional. As a result, Scott uses his Masters degree in Education and 15 years teaching experience to educate his clients as they begin to put their lives in order.

Scott is in demand as a time management coach, speaker and personal organizing instructor providing valuable counsel to a variety of residential and business clients. He was one of the nation's inaugural CPO® certification recipients, earning his designation in 2007. As an active member of the National Association of Professional Organizers (NAPO) since 2004, Scott has served as the President and Director of Technology for the Washington, DC—Metro Chapter of NAPO. In 2008, he was awarded Professional Organizer of the Year, the highest accolade given by his peers in NAPO—WDC. Scott has served as the Director of Technology for The Board of Certification for Professional Organizers, has a Chronic Disorganization Specialist Certificate from the National Study Group on Chronic Disorganization and is a member of NAPO's elite Golden Circle.

Get Organized for the **Planet**
Eliminating Your Clutter in an Eco-Friendly Way

By Nancy Castelli, CPO®

Getting organized is all about sustainability. Putting the "stuff" that doesn't serve you back out into the planet to serve someone else is simply the right thing to do. "What does getting organized have to do with the planet?" you may ask. Great question. Let me explain.

Everyone and everything on the planet is some form of matter and energy spinning together, evolving and all connected. Human beings are a lot of energy and a bit of matter. A tree, on the other hand, is more matter than energy. Let's take it even smaller now—down to those shoes in your closet. They, too, are bits of matter and energy—the energy of a tree for its wood, perhaps a cow for its leather and of course the human hands which formed them. Parts of this spinning earth came together to create a pair of shoes whose *purpose* is to protect your feet, allowing you to walk comfortably. When they are on your feet, supporting you, you give purpose to all the matter and energy that went into that pair of shoes. On the other hand, when they sit at the bottom of your closet, simply gathering dust, the purpose of those shoes is lost.

With this premise, I hope you can see how getting organized is all about sustainability. It's about making sure that the stuff that you have around you *supports* and *serves* you. If it doesn't, consider that it is actually bad for you and for our planet to hold on to possessions that could be out there serving someone else. All of the co-authors in this book can give you one reason or another to motivate you to get organized. Allow me to give you one more. Do it for the planet—to sustain this planet for all of our children and their children, and so on. I invite you to embrace this philosophy, make it your own and put some balance back into the planet. Turn matter into energy.

The Top 10 Best Ways to Eliminate Your Clutter Sustainably

To get you started, here is a countdown of the top ten easiest, sustainable ways to eliminate the things you have that aren't serving you. In reviewing these top ten, you will find that there are a limited number of local resources cited. When possible, I will cite national sources or Web-based sources, but most of the places available to you for the green elimination of your clutter will be right around the corner from where you live or work. Your favorite Web search engine makes it easy to find resources. Always look for options that are nearby, easy to get to or within route of your typical day. Discover the joy of giving back to your community by taking a little time to do some research for your best local options, with the guidance here to get you started.

10. Reduce, Reuse, Recycle

Commonly known as the three Rs, the reduce, reuse and recycle principle—in that order—is simply a way to live by producing less waste. You can have a major impact on the amount of trash that ends up in the landfills simply by changing your habits about buying, using and discarding your stuff. Embrace a more planet-friendly attitude by producing less waste in the first place. Practice the three

Rs by buying products that are less toxic or contain less packaging, using reusable containers and other reusable items, maintaining and repairing products, participating in recycling programs and buying products made from recycled materials.

First, reduce what you use, which starts in the store by buying less stuff. So important is the idea of reduction of use for sustainability that you will learn much more about this a little later when we get to #1.

Second, reuse or repurpose your stuff to extend its life. For example, if a container or bin can be used elsewhere, repurpose it instead of buying something new. The planet already gave a piece of itself up for that garbage pail. If you don't like how it looks in the bedroom, use it as a bucket in the garage. If you organized your receipts and no longer need that shoebox, use it inside a drawer as a divider. Be creative. There are many ways to reuse items that would otherwise go into the trash.

Finally, most of us understand that recycling means to process used items in order that the material can be used to make new products. Many people rely on recycling entirely, giving no thought to the idea of reducing and reusing. Don't fall into that complacent place. Be aware that in many municipalities, it is still a challenge to recycle and much of what goes into the recycling bins is still not effectively recycled. While it is great to recycle as much as possible, don't forget the front end by reducing and reusing wherever you can.

For example, you can go out and buy a bottle of water and then recycle it. However, that is not as good as using a bottle or container you already have over and over again. You reduced by not buying something new, reused an existing container and eliminated the need to recycle. Most importantly you decreased the need for the water bottling company to produce a new bottle of water to replace the one you just bought.

9. Find a Donation Center You Love

Most of us are familiar with the concept of donating possessions to a donation center. However, I still see people with bags of clothing and such that end up sitting stagnant in a corner as clutter. Make it easy to get these items out of your space and into a new space by having options.

- Have a donation box in every bedroom of the house so adults and children in the household get into the habit of filling it up when clothing and other household items are ready for a new home. This is a great way to start good habits with your children.

- Choose a donation source whose mission you value. That will motivate you and your loved ones to donate often. If you are a pet lover, find a pet organization that takes donations.

- Make sure that the donation center maintains hours that work with your busy schedule and is in an easy-to-get-to location near you. Ideally a place somewhere on your normal work or errand route or near a place you go often. That way it's easy to get these items out of your space and into the hands of someone else who can appreciate them.

The Salvation Army (www.salvationarmyusa.org) and Goodwill (www.goodwill.org) are great national sources that may have a location in your local area. Still, remember to explore local organizations you wish to support. You may end up with two or four favorite places to take the variety of your stuff (more ideas to follow). As it becomes a part of your routine, soon you will see how easy it is to visit those centers and serve the planet!

8. Share Your Entertainment Collections

There are many sources that can use your books, CDs and other entertainment possessions. In fact, in some instances you can even make money by donating this type of clutter. Used book and music stores will often give you money back or store credit for second-hand books, CDs and DVDs.

For music and instruments, check around your city or neighborhood for a music or art school. The young students in most of these institutions would love to reuse the musical instruments that are gathering dust in your home. Unfinished projects are clutter too. If you haven't yet taken those music lessons or haven't played that guitar in years, perhaps it's time to let it go to a dedicated student.

"Getting organized is all about sustainability. Putting the 'stuff' that doesn't serve you back out into the planet to serve someone else is simply the right thing to do."

7. Unload Your Extra Office Supplies

In the homes and offices I have organized, there is almost always an overstock of some type of office and craft supplies. We keep binders, half-used notebooks, pencils/pens/markers, colored paper and more, expecting that it might get used someday. Times have changed and it is very possible that you won't use all those overstock items. School-teachers, after-school programs or childcare centers, on the other hand, with their incredibly shrinking budgets could really use your office supplies and craft items today! Teachers have to fend for themselves to create that next art or craft activity for students and often have to use their own money to get the supplies. I have yet to come across a school that refuses this type of donation item. Eliminate your office supply clutter and serve your community school or childcare center.

6. Get Rid of Your Tech and Electronic Gear

New technology gadgets are fun and everyone wants to have the most current version. This means most of us end up with lots of dated tech and electronic gear. You can try to sell it on eBay or Craigslist. These are both great resources, but it does require you put aside the time to get it done—processing the transaction means email exchanges, phone calls, setting appointments, shipping it out and so on.

There is also another great way to get rid of your possibly valuable, but definitely toxic-to-the-planet, high tech devices and gadgets. Check out Gazelle (www.gazelle.com). At this site you can calculate the value of your gadgets and Gazelle will give you a quote and even send you a box or envelope to mail it to them, including prepaid postage! Gazelle will resell or recycle the product for you. While you might get a little less than you would on eBay or Craigslist, you won't spend nearly as much of your valuable time.

What do you do with all the tech gear and gadgets that don't work or the parts, pieces and components? Watch for local services that collect tech items. Schools and non-profit organizations often have weekend "tech collection days" to raise money or simply as a service. Also, check with nearby computer and electronics stores that often take these items. Finally, do a search on Earth 911 (www.earth911.com). If you can't find a local service, you can at least make a suggestion on this site to let them know you want a local service in your area.

Organizing for the Planet MUST KNOW website:
www.earth911.com

Earth 911 is an environmental services company that has consolidated environmental hotlines, web sites and other information sources nationwide into one convenient network. The site is well organized with a bevy of information to educate you on the 3 Rs and community-specific sources for your end-of-life items.

---

5. Discard Lotions, Potions and Notions, Including Meds

If you travel often, you may have a vast collection of unused hotel soap and shampoo samples. You may have only partially used lotions and soaps that you just didn't like. Most donation centers won't take your toiletries, especially if they have been opened and used. Instead, do a little research and find a nearby homeless or battered women's shelter. There are facilities like this everywhere. These places won't mind if you have an open bottle of shampoo or a half-used bottle of mouthwash you don't like. The people they serve can use these items either at the shelter or to start their new home. Make a call or two or ask around, keeping in mind that for obvious reasons, battered women's shelters in particular are prolific but usually discreet as to their location.

Now, about those unused or expired medications—first, please be advised that they are usually toxic to the planet. Flushing them down the toilet or putting them in the trash is not a good idea. You are poisoning your own land and water supply. Look for a hospital, medical facility or a drug store that will take your meds and reuse or dispose of them properly. Earth 911 may also provide a local source. See the "Must Know" box on the previous page for contact information. For supplements and vitamins, just dump them into the compost bin and recycle the bottle.

4. Get to Know Your Local Options for Trash and Recycling

Every municipality has programs for the elimination of waste and most cities are trying to expand and deliver even more planet-friendly options. I am privileged to live in San Francisco, where we have a plethora of great options when it comes to recycling, toxic waste elimination, composting and more. As a citizen, I get mail and information about those options and I read up. As a customer, I was

189

also able to actually go visit the waste facility and learn more details about the program and even tour the facility. What is available in your city or town? How can you learn more? I encourage you to find out and get savvy. The more you are educated about the trash, recycle and toxic waste services available to you, the more conscientious and motivated you will be to eliminate your waste and clutter.

If you find your city of residence has very few options in this regard, perhaps it's time for you and your neighbors to make some noise about it. It ultimately may end up costing you a little more money in local taxes but the future children of this planet will thank you.

3. Identify and Eliminate Toxic and Hazardous Waste

"Toxic chemicals in our environment threaten our rivers and lakes, our air, land, and oceans, and ultimately ourselves and our future."
—www.greenpeace.org

It's time to get educated on what toxic waste is and learn how to eliminate that waste. You might be surprised to learn how many choices there are for you to be responsible in this regard. For example, household batteries are very toxic yet surprisingly easy to eliminate safely. Many local hardware stores and Home Depots will gladly take your dead batteries. Yet, according to a recent survey on www.earth911.org, 70 percent of those surveyed said they either didn't know they could be recycled or didn't know how to do so.

How to eliminate hazardous waste depends upon your locale. Check your trash service to see if it has options for you or check www.earth911.com. The following is a list of typical household hazardous waste you can eliminate responsibly.

Hazardous waste which can be disposed of responsibly	
Medications	Latex paint
Batteries	Oil paint and other finishes
Fuels	Solvents and thinners
Electronics	Asbestos
Technology gear, computers, mobile phones	Cleaning solutions, including ammonia, bleach, TSP, all-purpose cleaners, metal polish
Aerosols	
Fluorescent tubes, CFLs	Used cooking oil
Pesticides and other garden chemicals	Fire extinguishers
	Roofing tar and adhesives
Mercury	Used motor oil and auto products
Ammunition, explosives	Photographic chemicals
Road flares	Pool chemicals

2. Build a Home Recycling Center

For those of us challenged with clutter issues, the problem may begin because we are very busy people. If something isn't easy to do and systems aren't in place, clutter accumulates. A great way to make the practice of disposing of your green clutter easy is to build a Home Recycling Center. A great location for this is in the garage, the kitchen or the entrance area of your home. A shelving system or cabinet with wide and deep shelves is best. Get, or better still, repurpose bins and label them. Bins of all sizes can be used, depending on the category. The following is a partial list of the typical kinds of categories for which you will want bins:

- Recycle—separate ones for paper, plastic, cans, etc., if necessary
- Toxic waste
- Donation items

- Office and craft supplies

- Books

- CDs, DVDs

- Tech/electronics

- Medication

- Glasses/optical wear

- Lotions/potions/soaps

- Terracycle brigade—see chart below

Get the whole household involved in building a center, contributing to it, and disposing of the recyclable items. For more information, the University of Iowa has published a great two-page document entitled "Create a Home Recycling Center." If you can't find it online, I have it posted on my website in the Tool Box section at www.balancesf.com.

> ## Organizing for the Planet MUST KNOW website:
> ## www.terracycle.net
>
> Terracycle is an extraordinary operation that turns "trash" into useable stuff. Send them your juice bags, for example, and they will turn them into colorful purses and pencil cases and resell them at Target or Walgreens. They'll even donate money to your charity of choice for each item you send them. Start or join a "brigade" and start recycling your trash.

And now for the number one best way to eliminate your clutter sustainably:

1. Stop Shopping!

This may be the most difficult, yet ultimately the most important way for you to reduce your clutter and serve the planet at the same time. For many of my clients, buying too much is a big reason for clutter in the first place. It's a challenge, because we are living in a consumerist world with a "he who dies with the most stuff wins" philosophy. By embracing sustainability and the idea of serving your planet, you will covet the idea of reducing the size of your "footprint," in this case, the amount of stuff you have.

One idea is to choose one month of the year (or one quarter or even an entire year) where you simply do not buy anything at all except consumable items like food and toilet paper. For that period of time, make do with what you already own. No new books or magazines; read what you have. No new shoes or clothing; wear what's already in your closet. No new furniture or household items; enjoy your current décor. You might be surprised how easy it is. Perhaps you will even rediscover old stuff that you have missed or forgotten you had.

If you need more encouragement, I highly recommend you watch a 20-minute online animation of the consumerist society called, "The Story of Stuff" narrated by Anne Leonard (www.storyofstuff.com). It may just raise your ire enough to make this no shopping idea really easy.

On the days when you are allowing yourself to shop, be a little bit more conscientious about it. Many professional organizers will tell you about the "one in-one out" method. That means that when you are ready to buy a new pair of shoes, for example, you know that when you go home, you have to get rid of an old pair of shoes. If you aren't ready to do that, then walk away from the register.

Turning Matter into Energy

I come back to my philosophy that everything around us on this beautiful spinning Mother Earth is some form of matter and energy. And guess what? Clutter is a big chunk of heavy, negative matter. How is clutter supporting you in your life? Indeed, it is not. When you consider your own clutter, consider this: that pile of paper wants a purpose; that closet full of who knows what is not serving anyone. Get busy making decisions about your stuff. Is it active and serving you in your life? If it isn't, get it out of your space and off to serve someone else. Reduce, reuse, recycle—it's good for you and it's good for the planet. Turn matter—your clutter and disorder—into positive energy where everything is in its place waiting to serve you.

NANCY CASTELLI, CPO®
BALANCE Organizing Services Company

Turning matter into energy

(415) 821-9021
nancy@balancesf.com
www.balancesf.com

Nancy Castelli is a professional organizer and productivity consultant. She has 18 years experience in organizing, speaking and time/project management from her former career in the corporate world. In 2005, she launched her own company, BALANCE Organizing Services. She helps professionals, entrepreneurs, busy moms and even children turn their matter (clutter and disorder) into energy (where everything is in its place, waiting to serve). Her one-on-one consulting practice is a combination of coaching and hands-on organizing through which her clients experience life changes that result in living a more productive and balanced life.

As part of her organizing practice, Nancy conducts workshops to educate and motivate those frustrated with clutter and disorder. Attendees are empowered with a habit-altering philosophy and leave with real-life tips and tools for getting organized. She also serves the community through customized, organizing-oriented motivational speaking engagements. Nancy is an active member of the National Association of Professional Organizers (NAPO), Business Network International (BNI) and the San Francisco Chamber of Commerce. She holds a B.S. from Bowling Green State University.

Disasters Happen—
Organize for **Action** Now
By JoAnn Scordino, CEM

Preparing for the unexpected emergency or disaster can easily be a part of organizing your life affairs. As you are clearing your clutter and putting order to your environment, include getting prepared for the unexpected. This chapter will give you simple steps to upgrading your safety net for yourself and loved ones, your home, your workplace and your community.

According to the National Citizens Corps program, on average:

- In 95 percent of all emergencies, bystanders or victims themselves are the first to provide emergency assistance or to perform a rescue.
- There is one firefighter for every 265 people.
- There is one law enforcement officer for every 334 people.
- There is one paramedic/EMT for every 325 people.

On an average day in most communities in the United States, our system works. The great disparity between formal emergency personnel and citizens is fairly transparent to the majority of us. Those odds greatly increase against us for receiving professional help in larger scale events.

"Emergencies" can be defined as single incidents which are easily handled by our normal daily emergency response service agencies. A "disaster" is when there are multiple emergencies occurring simultaneously or a wide segment of a community has been impacted. A "catastrophic disaster" is one where the devastation is so huge and widespread that it requires immediate local, state and national assistance. Hurricane Katrina and September 11, 2001 are the greatest catastrophic events on American soil to date in the twenty-first century.

Natural disasters tend to be our greatest threats—earthquakes, fires, floods, hurricanes, tornadoes, volcanic eruptions, tsunamis, pandemics and extreme weather conditions. Human-made disasters can include terrorism (nuclear, biological or chemical), airplane crashes and utility disruptions, to name a few.

Who to Prepare for the Unexpected

The reality is, you don't know where you will be when a disaster strikes or if you will be the one giving or receiving support. That's why it is vital to take responsibility and get prepared and trained for the unexpected.

Take a moment and think about who matters most to you—your family and friends, your children or elders, your pets, your neighbors and your community.

When to Prepare for the Unexpected

The time to prepare is now—not tomorrow or someday, but now. Take it a step at a time, so as to not become overwhelmed and discouraged. Make this a team effort or pick a buddy. Partnership makes a difference.

When you take actions to prepare yourself, you exercise the muscle of preparedness. When you plan with your family, co-workers, neighbors and community groups, you exercise your team muscle of preparedness. This keeps you in shape and ready to respond if and when disaster strikes.

For every hour you spend preparing, you will save yourself at least 10-20 hours after disaster strikes. There is truly no time to waste—now is the right time to begin to prepare.

What to Prepare for the Unexpected

Listed are specific actions and items for you to prepare for the unexpected. The industry standard of "Get a Kit, Make a Plan, Be Informed" promoted by FEMA (Federal Emergency Management Agency) and the American Red Cross is good. I cover and recommend the same actions, items and plans—my approach is simply more personalized.

1. Your identity. One of the first things people fear losing when an emergency happens are their key identification records. If you were to lose documents or records, which ones would be the most vital to your identity and the most difficult to recreate? Here's a short list. Please fill in the gaps for your specific needs.

Organizing your vital identity documents checklist:

- Driver's license

- Social Security card

- Passport

- Birth certificate

- Medical info—allergies, medications/dosages, doctor contacts, health history

- Insurance policies and cards

- Family photos for identification purposes
- Financial records—bank accounts, stock, bond certificates and so on
- Legal documents—will, health directives and the like
- Deed or mortgage documents
- Inventory and photographs of your valuables
- Any other documents that would be difficult to replace—work permits, adoption papers and so on

Be sure to make a backup copy of all your identity cards and vital documents that could be lost. Date and store a copy for yourself, send one to your out-of-state contact person and/or place a copy in a safety deposit box. It is essential that you have copies stored off-site.

2. Your relationships. If disaster were to strike now, who are the people in your life you would want informed of your situation? It is vital to make a plan now for who and how you want those closest to you contacted. Also, we live in a time when news in our world is reported immediately and the communication systems, if not downed, become overloaded with calls in and out of the impacted area. Emergency personnel need the communication lines first to save lives and property. It is our responsibility to not burden the system further and to have a plan to let those closest to us know of our status.

Organizing your vital relationships checklist:

- Select a close family member or friend to be your spokesperson. This person should live a distance from you, preferably out of state.
- Give your spokesperson a contact list of the important people in your life.

- Give every member of your family an emergency card with your key contact information.

- Use your emergency out-of-state contact person to help reunite separated family members and communicate special medical needs of family members.

- Give them copies of your important documents to store, if appropriate.

- Plan to use a variety of communication tools, such as landlines, cell phones, email and social media sites.

3. Your valuables. Our homes, our valuables and items of comfort are vital to our lives. If your home were damaged or destroyed by an emergency or disaster, do you know what you have? Do you have a record of your life possessions for insurance documentation? Do you have sufficient insurance coverage for your current valuables? These are all things to consider when organizing for the unexpected.

Creating an inventory of your life valuables may seem too overwhelming of a project with your busy life. Here's my professional advice as an organizer: document the bigger picture items first, and then add the smaller items if and when time allows. For example, if you have several hundred books or CDs, list how many and take photos for proof and to jog your memory. If and when you have time later, catalogue the details. Always date the version and store copies off-site immediately. You can update later!

- Create an inventory of your valuables—home and business.

- Make a list, take photographs or make a video of your home contents and valuables.

- Make duplicate copies of the inventory list, photos or video to be stored off-site.

- Always date your documentation so updated versions can easily be identified.

- Store your inventory list, photos or video with your vital documents off-site and/or in a safety deposit box.

- Check with your insurance company to see if your current coverage is sufficient and if it has any inventory requirements.

4. Your plan. Organize your household emergency plan and include communications, supply kits, evacuation plans and alternate meeting sites. As a family, discuss in advance what you need to do to prepare for an emergency and explain the potential dangers to children and others in your care. Make special plans and provisions for your children, elders, persons with disabilities, service animals and your family pets. Include everyone and plan to share responsibilities and work together as a team.

Organizing your household plan checklist:

- Post emergency telephone numbers in a central location and give everyone a pocket copy to carry (fire, police, key contacts).

- Teach children how and when to call 911.

- Look for possible hazards in your home, particularly things that might fall from high places, remove heavy objects from above beds, clear exit ways and so on.

- Have up-to-date fire extinguishers and know how and when to use them.

- Install smoke detectors on each level of your home, especially near bedrooms. Check and replace batteries regularly.

- Teach able family members when and how to turn off the water, gas, and electricity.

- Identify safe spots in your home for each type of disaster.
- Identify all possible ways to exit your home in an emergency.
- Determine alternate evacuation routes and a meeting spot in your neighborhood.
- Identify an alternate location for everyone to meet a distance from your home, if you are not able to get home or must evacuate the area.
- Have a plan and provisions for those with special needs—children, elders, people with disabilities, people of various languages, pets.
- Secure your home. Bolt heavy objects and furniture to the walls, install cabinet latches, identify secure rooms for severe weather situations, raise your home in flood prone areas, bolt your home to its foundation for earthquakes.
- Practice and update your plan regularly.

5. Your supplies. Organize emergency supplies for your home, car or workplace. Most of us already have a number of the recommended items; it is a matter of gathering them into kits and key locations to have immediate access to them if an emergency occurs.

The industry standard recommends that you prepare for 72 hours (three days). For your car or workplace, a three-day supply is appropriate. For your home, we strongly suggest that you prepare at least one week's worth of supplies. Think of this as preparing to survive as opposed to the expectation that in a few hours or days all of your individual needs will be met by an outside source. As we have all seen repeatedly when large scale disasters occur, it could take days to weeks to have services restored. Prepare for longer—it will make you stronger.

Organizing your vital emergency supplies:

- Drinking water—at least one gallon per person, per day. Water is your most essential item to stay alive and hydrated. Be sure to replace your emergency water supply every six months to a year.

- Food—non-perishable that doesn't need refrigeration, cooking or water. Be sure to include a manual can opener.

- Medical supplies & prescriptions—be sure to have a sufficient supply, especially for medical conditions that would be life threatening.

- First aid kits.

- Flashlights, extra batteries and whistles. For safety reasons do NOT use candles.

- Sanitation supplies.

- Heavy work gloves for picking up debris or chemicals.

- Duct tape, tools and so on.

- Sturdy walking shoes and protective clothing.

- Items for those with special needs—children, elders, persons with disabilities and pets.

- Emergency cash and change.

- Copies of your vital documents, inventory and contacts.

We highly recommend you check your supplies and replenish perishable items such as water, food, medicines, batteries, and so on, at least one time a year. A good reminder is in the fall or spring when the time changes.

This list is not comprehensive and may not meet all your needs in an emergency situation. Please refer to the preparedness sites listed under "Your Community and Resources" for more detailed lists.

6. Your community and resources. Get involved, get trained and be prepared to help yourself and others, no matter where you are. One of the best training programs available throughout the United States is the Community Emergency Response Team (CERT) program. You will get trained in how to take care of yourself, assist others and volunteer in your community before and after disasters.

There are *many* disaster preparedness resources available to us. Listed here are a few of the most noteworthy national preparedness websites.

- The FEMA website at www.ready.gov is informative and user-friendly.
- The National Citizen Corps Program at www.citizencorps.gov has great information on how to get trained and volunteer in your community.
- The Community Emergency Response Team (CERT) training is outstanding. To find it in your community, go to www.citizencorps.gov/cert.
- The American Red Cross website is www.redcross.org.
- The National Fire Protection Association is at www.nfpa.org.
- The Center for Disease Control and Prevention is at www.cdc.gov.
- The National Weather Service is at www.nws.noaa.gov.
- The United States Geological Survey is at www.usgs.gov.

Preparing for the Unexpected Is a Process

All emergencies and disasters happen at the local level. First, local responders and resources are used and if the situation merits it, the mayor or top city official may make a local declaration of disaster. Once that is done, if the situation is larger than what the local resources can handle, the local official may appeal to the governor for state assistance and resources. Once granted, if the state resources are also overwhelmed, the governor may make a request to the President of the United States for federal assistance. If a presidential declaration of disaster is granted, then FEMA is called into action. Typically, this can take many days to get the declaration signed and to mobilize federal resources into the affected area.

As citizens, we have a perception and expectation that our government should be right there on the ground when a disaster happens. However, our emergency response system is not structured that way. First on the ground when disaster strikes are everyday citizens, like you and me. Give yourself, your loved ones and your community the ultimate gift of preparing for the unexpected. Organize for action *now*.

JOANN SCORDINO, CEM
Organize for Action

Get real, get ready—
disaster preparedness planning

(415) 474-9140
info@organizeforaction.com
www.organizeforaction.com

As a consultant, JoAnn Scordino has been called the "Czarina of disaster preparedness." She evolved from being a professional wardrobe organizer to the go-to gal for crisis management. In the mid-1980s, JoAnn started her business, Organize for Action, and became a founding member of the San Francisco/Bay Area, National Association of Professional Organizers (NAPO).

From 1995 to 2005, JoAnn worked for the San Francisco Mayor's Office of Emergency Services as the Community Disaster Preparedness Coordinator, delivering preparedness presentations to over 20,000 participants. On September 11, 2001, she was responsible for activating the key players and Emergency Operations Center in San Francisco. JoAnn also worked in Louisiana on the 2006 post Hurricane Katrina evacuation plan. Through the International Association of Emergency Managers, JoAnn is a credentialed Certified Emergency Manager (CEM) and serves on their Special Needs Caucus.

JoAnn's commitment to educate the public about being prepared is her life's passion. She believes in inspiring the average citizen to get real and to get ready. JoAnn is an experienced consultant with a unique ability to refine complicated information in a simple and direct way. She is a frequently requested motivational presenter at domestic and international conferences.

More Get Organized TODAY

Now that you have learned how to organize your life in a variety of ways, the next step is to take action. Get started applying what you have learned in the pages of this book.

We want you to know that we are here to help you meet your professional and personal objectives.

Following is a list of where we are geographically located. Regardless of where our companies are located, many of us provide a variety of services over the phone or through webinars and we welcome the opportunity to travel to your location.

You can find out more about each of us by reading our bios at the end of our chapters or by visiting our websites listed on the next two pages.

When you are ready for one-on-one consulting or group training from any of the co-authors in this book—we are available! If you call us and let us know you have read our book, we will provide you with a free phone consultation to determine your needs and how to best serve you.

Arizona

Charlotte Steill, CPO®   www.simplyputorganizing.com

California

Toni Ahlgren   www.clearlyorg.com
Nancy Castelli, CPO®   www.balancesf.com
Rhonda Elliott   www.organizedbydesign.biz
Bibi Goldstein   www.buyingtimellc.com
JoAnn Scordino, CEM   www.organizeforaction.com
Melissa Stacey   www.feelingorganized.com
Sandy Stelter, JD, CPO®   www.sos2day.com
Angela F. Wallace, MIA, CPO®   www.wallaceassociates.net

Florida

Tina Oscar   www.smartkitchentips.com

Minnesota

Gretchen Ditto   www.dittoandco.com
Annette Watz, MARE, CDC   www.watzthebigidea.com

Ohio

Mary L. Noble, CDC   www.empoweryourdreamer.com

Oregon

Anne Blumer, CPO®   www.solutionsforyou.com

Pennsylvania

Anna Sicalides, CPO®   www.annaorganizesu.com

Virginia

Janet Schiesl   www.basicorganization.com

Washington

Katie Munoz   www.movingforwardinc.com
Natasha Packer   www.organizingasyouwish.com

Washington, DC

Scott Roewer, CPO®   www.solutionsbyscott.com

PowerDynamics PUBLISHING

PowerDynamics Publishing develops books for experts who want to share their knowledge with more and more people.
We provide our co-authors with a proven system, professional guidance and support, producing quality, multi-author, how-to books that uplift and enhance the personal and professional lives of the people they serve.

We know that getting a book written and published is a huge undertaking. To make that process as easy as possible, we have an experienced team with the resources and know-how to put a quality, informative book in the hands of our co-authors quickly and affordably. Our co-authors are proud to be included in PowerDynamics Publishing books because these publications enhance their business missions, give them a professional outreach tool and enable them to communicate essential information to a wider audience.

You can find out more about our upcoming book projects at
www.powerdynamicspub.com

Also from
PowerDynamics Publishing

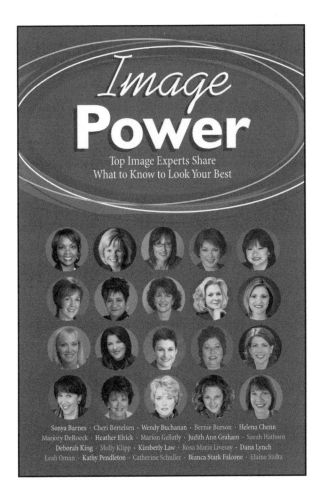

For more information on this book, visit:
www.imagepowerbook.com

Also from
PowerDynamics Publishing

Top Image Experts Share What to Know to Advance Your Career

EXECUTIVE
IMAGE
POWER

Colleen Abrie · Yasmin Anderson-Smith · Ginny Baldridge · Joanne Blake · Jennifer Bressie
Karen Brunger · Amy Elizabeth Casson · Betty Chu · Julie Kaufman · Kathryn Lowell
Suzanne Mauro · Maureen Merrill · Brenda Moore-Frazier · Peggy M. Parks · Beverly Samuel
Lauren Solomon · Anne Sowden · Beth Thorp · Divya Vashi · Cynthia Bruno Wynkoop

For more information on this book, visit:
www.executiveimagebook.com

Also from
PowerDynamics Publishing

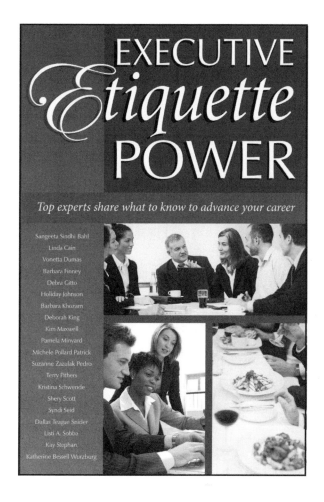

For more information on this book, visit:
www.execetiquette.com

Also from
PowerDynamics Publishing

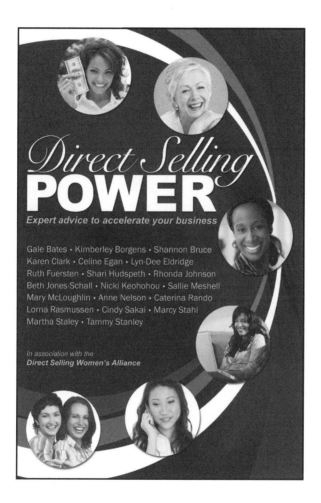

For more information on this book, visit:
www.directsellingpower.com

Also from
PowerDynamics Publishing

TOP IMAGE EXPERTS
reveal strategies to always
look and be your best

INSPIRED
Style

Ginny Baldridge · Michele Bayle · Shirley Borrelli · Mari Bowlin
Chris Fulkerson · Pat Gray · Milena Joy · Barbara Layne · Carrie Leum
Julie Maeder · Lisa Ann Martin · Teresa McCarthy · Cynthia Lee Miller
Oreet Mizrahi · Sandy Moore · Cheryl Obermiller · Deborah Reynolds
Sally Templeton · Dominique Vaughan-Russell · Alison Vaughn · Debbie Wright

For more information on this book, visit:
www.inspiredstylebook.com